WORKBOOK

ENTREPRENEURSHIP
How to Start & Operate a Small Business

A Guide for THE YOUNG ENTREPRENEUR

Tenth Revised Edition

STEVE MARIOTTI,
President and Founder of the National Foundation for Teaching Entrepreneurship, Inc. (NFTE)

with Laurie Wendell and Peter McBride

Copyright © 1987, 1994, 1997, 2001, 2003 & 2006 by
The National Foundation for Teaching Entrepreneurship, Inc. (NFTE)
120 Wall Street, 29th Floor, New York, NY 10005.

Special thanks to Jackson Mariotti, Nina Mariotti, Siena Mariotti, and Spencer Mariotti, as well as Julia Vlock for their help reviewing this material.

Royalty-free photographic images used in this publication are copyright of Alamy Limited (cover).

Any reproduction, in whole or in part, by any means, without express written permission, is prohibited.

Printed in the United States of America.

ISBN 1-890859-19-2
4 5 6 7 08 07

Table of Contents

To the Student iv

Basic Module: Starting Your Business (Chapters 1-16)

    Unit 1   What Is an Entrepreneur? (Chapters 1-6)
              Chapter 1: What Is Entrepreneurship? 1
              Chapter 2: The Building Block of Business 7
              Chapter 3: Return on Investment 13
              Chapter 4: Opportunity Recognition 19
              Chapter 5: Characteristics of the Successful Entrepreneur 29
              Chapter 6: Supply and Demand 35

    Unit 2   What Business Would You Like to Start? (Chapters 7-11)
              Chapter 7: Inventions and Product Development 41
              Chapter 8: Selecting Your Business 47
              Chapter 9: Costs of Running a Business 53
              Chapter 10: What Is Marketing? 59
              Chapter 11: Market Research 65

    Unit 3   Show Me the Money! Tracking Costs and Cash (Chapters 12-16)
              Chapter 12: Keeping Good Records 71
              Chapter 13: Income Statements 83
              Chapter 14: Financing Strategy 89
              Chapter 15: Negotiation 95
              Chapter 16: From the Wholesaler to the Trade Fair 101

    Basic Module: *Business Plan Review* 105

Intermediate Module: Operating Your Business (Chapters 17-30)

    Unit 4   Marketing: Who Are Your Customers/What Will They Buy? (Chapters 17-20)
              Chapter 17: Competitive Strategy 121
              Chapter 18: Developing Your Marketing Mix 129
              Chapter 19: Advertising and Publicity 135
              Chapter 20: Break-Even Analysis 143

    Unit 5   Selling, Customer Service, Communication (Chapters 21-24)
              Chapter 21: Principles of Successful Selling 147
              Chapter 22: Customer Service 153
              Chapter 23: Math Tips to Help You Sell and Negotiate 157
              Chapter 24: Business Communication 161

    Unit 6   Operating a Small Business (Chapters 25-30)
              Chapter 25: Sole Proprietorships and Partnerships 167
              Chapter 26: Manufacturing 173
              Chapter 27: The Production/Distribution Chain 179
              Chapter 28: Quality 185
              Chapter 29: Effective Leadership 191
              Chapter 30: Technology 201

    Intermediate Module: *Business Plan Review* 209

Advanced Module: What You Need to Know to Grow (Chapters 31-50)

    Unit 7   Financing Your Business (Chapters 31-36)
            Chapter 31: Finding Sources of Capital 227
            Chapter 32: Corporations 233
            Chapter 33: Stocks 239
            Chapter 34: Bonds 247
            Chapter 35: The Balance Sheet 251
            Chapter 36: Venture Capital 259

    Unit 8   Building Strong Business Relationships (Chapters 37-40)
            Chapter 37: Contracts 265
            Chapter 38: Socially Responsible Business and Philanthropy 273
            Chapter 39: Small Business and Government 281
            Chapter 40: Building Good Personal and Business Credit 287

    Unit 9   Protecting Your Business (Chapters 41-45)
            Chapter 41: Cash Flow 293
            Chapter 42: Protecting Intellectual Property 299
            Chapter 43: Ethical Business Behavior 305
            Chapter 44: Taxation and the Entrepreneur 313
            Chapter 45: Insurance 317

    Unit 10   Creating Wealth (Chapters 46-50)
            Chapter 46: Franchising and Licensing 323
            Chapter 47: International Opportunities 329
            Chapter 48: Investment Goals and Risk Tolerance 335
            Chapter 49: Investing for a Secure Future 341
            Chapter 50: Exit Strategies 347

    Advanced Module: *Business Plan Review* 351

Sample Student Business Plans 363
    Basic Sample Student Business Plan 364
    Intermediate Sample Student Business Plan 376
    Advanced Sample Student Business Plan *(pages 586-612 of student text)*

Basic Business Plan Template 399
Intermediate Business Plan Template 415
Advanced Business Plan Template 433

NFTE Record Keeping System 445

For information regarding NFTE programs and products, contact
(212) 232-3333 or (800) FOR-NFTE; fax: (212) 232-2244; www.nfte.com

To the Student

This workbook contains all of the student activities for the Basic, Intermediate, and Advanced modules in the student textbook — plus more! These exercises and activities correspond, on a chapter-by-chapter basis, with the material covered in your textbook. As you go through the exercises, look back at your textbook to help you answer the questions. Also included in this workbook is the NFTE Record Keeping System.

In addition, your workbook contains three business plan reviews for you to complete. Your business plan is your ticket to starting your own, successful business, so writing a good plan is very important. After you have completed Chapter 16 in the textbook and workbook, you will be ready to write your Basic Business Plan. After Chapter 30, you will be ready to write your Intermediate Business Plan. After Chapter 50, you will be ready to write your Advanced Business Plan. Additionally, sample student business plans and a business plan template are available at the end of this workbook to assist you.

Remember, YOU can be an entrepreneur and start your own business! Good luck!

To learn more about The National Foundation for Teaching Entrepreneurship (NFTE), please visit www.nfte.com or call 1-800-FOR.NFTE.

WHAT IS ENTREPRENEURSHIP?

CRITICAL THINKING ABOUT... ENTREPRENEURSHIP

1. What would be the best thing about owning your own business?

2. What would be the worst?

3. Would you rather be an employee or an entrepreneur? Why?

4. Describe an idea for a business. Explain how it could satisfy a consumer need.

5. Go on the Internet and research "entrepreneurship." Write briefly about the most interesting site you found.

CHAPTER 1   WHAT IS ENTREPRENEURSHIP?

6. "Employees get paid what they deserve, but entrepreneurs don't." Explain this statement.

___

7. Identity three non-financial benefits of entrepreneurship that might be important to you. Write a paragraph on each explaining why. Use separate paper if you need more space.

___

8. Anita Roddick (The Body Shop), John Johnson (BET Holdings), Berry Gordy (Motown Records), Oprah Winfrey (Harpo), and Debbie Fields (Mrs. Fields Original Cookies) are all famous entrepreneurs. Make a list of the obstacles each of them faced in becoming the CEO of a major corporation. (Refer to Entrepreneurs in Profile to learn about them.) Use separate paper if you need more space.

___

9.

Business	Yearly Net Profit
Sal's Pizzeria:	$65,000
Books 'n' Things:	$123,000
Office Plantcare:	$1,100,175

Figure the selling price for these businesses, assuming each could be sold for three times yearly net profit.

KEY CONCEPTS

1. What is one thing all employees have in common?

2. Give a definition of "small business."

3. Even if your enterprise fails, what will you have gained?

4. Explain how profit works as a signal to the entrepreneur.

CHAPTER 1 WHAT IS ENTREPRENEURSHIP?

5. Do you agree that it will probably take about three months for your business to start earning a profit? Why or why not?
   _____
   _____
   _____

6. Describe three things you've learned about capitalism.
   _____
   _____
   _____
   _____

VOCABULARY

Write five sentences, using one or more of the following vocabulary words in each sentence. You might write about your family or your neighborhood. **Example:** My father is an *employee* of Baxter Shipping Company.

business ■ capital ■ capitalism ■ economy ■ employee ■ entrepreneur ■ free enterprise system ■ profit ■ resource ■ voluntary exchange

1. _____
   _____

2. _____
   _____

3. _____
   _____

4. _____
   _____

5. _____
   _____

MODULE 1   UNIT 1

CHAPTER 1 QUIZ
What Is Entrepreneurship?

1. What is the difference between an employee and an entrepreneur?
   _____
   _____
   _____
   _____
   _____
   _____
   _____
   _____
   _____
   _____
   _____
   _____
   _____
   _____
   _____

For the following advantages or disadvantages of being an entrepreneur, write A or D in the spaces below.

2. _____ Works long hours and often every day.

3. _____ Has a chance to acquire great wealth.

4. _____ May go bankrupt.

5. _____ Can't be laid off (fired).

6. _____ Has independence.

CHAPTER 1   WHAT IS ENTREPRENEURSHIP?

7. A small business has less than _____ employees.

   a. 1000

   b. 100

   c. 10

8. Should an entrepreneur give up if the first business fails? Explain.

   _____
   _____
   _____
   _____
   _____
   _____
   _____
   _____
   _____
   _____
   _____
   _____
   _____

THE BUILDING BLOCK OF BUSINESS:
The Economics of One Unit of Sale

CRITICAL THINKING ABOUT... THE BUILDING BLOCK OF BUSINESS

1. If you start a successful business, how will you spend your time? How would you want to be paid? (Hint: Choose one of the four options described in the chapter.) Explain.

2. What are your personal goals for the next five years? What do you hope to accomplish? Write a one-sentence "vision statement" that describes what you would like to achieve over the next five years.

KEY CONCEPTS

1. Gross profit is a business's profit before which other costs are subtracted?

2. What is the average unit of sale for the following businesses:

   a. A restaurant that serves $600 per day in meals to 60 customers (the average cost of goods sold per unit is $5.00)?

b. A record store that sells $1,000 worth of CDs per day to 40 customers (the average cost of goods sold per unit is $12.50)?

For the following businesses, define the unit of sale and determine the gross profit per unit.

3. Pete, the owner of The Funky DJ, provides DJ services to parties and other social events in his neighborhood. He charges $40 per hour. He rents a double turntable from his older brother at $10 per hour every time he works.

4. Sue, of Sue's Sandwich Shoppe, sells sandwiches and sodas from a sidewalk cart in a popular park near her house. She sets up her cart in the summers to raise money for college. Last month she sold $1,000 worth of _product_ (sandwiches and sodas) to 100 customers. Her unit is one sandwich (COGS $4) plus one soda (COGS $1). Total COGS = $5.00.

EXPLORATION

Locate and interview three entrepreneurs in your community. Ask each the questions below. Make up your own questions, too. Do you see anything these entrepreneurs have in common? Create a report or chart summarizing how they compare to one another.

1. Tell me what your business is about. [This will help you get context to understand the other answers better.]

MODULE 1   UNIT 1

2. What do you value most about being an entrepreneur?

_____
_____
_____
_____

3. Do you think your business will continue to grow?

_____
_____
_____
_____

4. Do you travel for your business? If so, where have you gone, and why? Did you enjoy it?

_____
_____
_____
_____

5. Do you think other people appreciate what you do? If so, what kinds of people, and why? [They don't have to be identified by name.]

_____
_____
_____
_____

6. What are your views about business failure? Have you ever experienced failure? What happened?

_____
_____
_____
_____

CHAPTER 2 — THE BUILDING BLOCK OF BUSINESS: The Economics of One Unit of Sale

7. If you could "live life over," would you choose to be an entrepreneur again, or would you choose something else?

   _____

   _____

   _____

   _____

VOCABULARY

Match the vocabulary word to its correct definition.

a. cost of goods sold
b. economics of one unit of sale (EOU)
c. gross profit
d. unit of sale

1. _____ one unit of the product or service a business sells
2. _____ the cost of selling "one additional unit"
3. _____ system of determining profits and costs for each unit of sale
4. _____ revenue minus cost of goods sold

CHAPTER 2 QUIZ
The Building Block of Business: The Economics of One Unit of Sale

1. Why should entrepreneurs study the economics of one unit of sale for their businesses?

2. List two ways an entrepreneur is paid.

3. What five breakthrough steps can entrepreneurs take to promote themselves?

4. What is included in the cost of goods sold for a manufacturer?

5. What is included in the cost of goods sold for a retailer?

6. What happens if an entrepreneur is directly involved in making a product but does not include his/her labor in the economics of one unit?

CHAPTER 2 THE BUILDING BLOCK OF BUSINESS: The Economics of One Unit of Sale

7. What is the unit of sale for a barber?
   _____
   _____
   _____

8. What is the average sale per customer for a restaurant that serves 200 customers a day and takes in sales revenue of $3,000?
   _____
   _____
   _____

9. You buy posters of celebrities from a wholesaler at $3 per poster, poster frames for $7 each from a different wholesaler, and sell the framed posters for $20. What is your gross profit?
   _____
   _____
   _____

10. You make fliers to help promote other young people's businesses. Each flier "package" includes three hours of design work plus 20 minutes of copying time at $15 per hour, plus 100 sheets of paper at 2 cents per sheet, plus $3 worth of other supplies. You sell each package for $100. What is your gross profit?
    _____
    _____
    _____

RETURN ON INVESTMENT:
Evaluating Education, Work, and Business

CRITICAL THINKING ABOUT... ROI

1. Complete the chart below. Assume a one-year investment period.

RETURN ON INVESTMENT (ROI)		
Net Profit	Investment	ROI
$4	$ _____	100%
30	60	_____ %
25	100	_____ %
4	10	_____ %
10	_____	33%
4,000	_____	40%
2,000	_____	200%
_____	20,000	6%

2. Describe a business you would like to start. What would your short-term goals be? (Short-term goals are returns on investment you would hope to see in one year.) What would your long-term goals be for the business? (These are goals that would take from one to five years to reach.)

_____
_____
_____
_____

3. What is your overall career goal? How much money do you expect to earn each year from your career?

_____
_____
_____
_____

CHAPTER 3 RETURN ON INVESTMENT: Evaluating Education, Work, and Business

4. How much education will you need to achieve your career goal? (Hint: Ask teacher or parents, or do research online.)
   _____
   _____

5. Use the "Rule of 72" to find the approximate number of years needed to double your money at the following rates of growth:
   a. 3% _____
   b. 5% _____
   c. 7% _____
   d. 18% _____
   e. 24% _____

KEY CONCEPTS

1. What is another term for "rate of return"?
   _____
   _____

2. How do you convert a decimal into a percentage?
   _____
   _____

3. What is the "quick way" to convert a decimal into a percentage?
   _____
   _____

4. Why can businesses started by young people face a lower risk of failure than adult businesses?

_____
_____
_____

5. What else can be invested besides money?

_____
_____
_____

IN YOUR OPINION

What would be the acceptable return to you for investing your time, energy, or money in the following? (Note: Your return does not have to be financial.)

1. Baby-sit a neighbor's child for two hours.

_____
_____
_____

2. Help your mother with the laundry.

_____
_____
_____

3. Do an hour of volunteer work at a hospital.

_____
_____
_____

4. Loan a friend $20 to start a candy business.

_____
_____
_____

CHAPTER 3 RETURN ON INVESTMENT: Evaluating Education, Work, and Business

VOCABULARY

Write five sentences about a business you would like to own. Use one or more of the following vocabulary words in each sentence. **Example:** I won't be able to hire employees right away, so I plan to invest a lot of *sweat equity*.

goal ■ interest rate ■ investment ■ percentage ■ rate of return ■ return on investment (ROI) ■ risk ■ Rule of 72 ■ sweat equity

1. _____

2. _____

3. _____

4. _____

5. _____

MODULE 1   UNIT 1

CHAPTER 3 QUIZ
Return on Investment: Evaluating Education, Work, and Business

1. What is the return on investment if a person invests $100 and gets back $150?
   _____
   _____
   _____

2. Why is starting to save or to invest early a good idea?
   _____
   _____
   _____
   _____
   _____

3. How much interest will be earned on $1,000 invested for one year at 6%?
   _____
   _____
   _____

4. Why can businesses started by young people stand a better chance of success than adult businesses?
   _____
   _____
   _____

5. Money is one type of investment. Name two other things people should invest in.
   _____
   _____
   _____
   _____
   _____

CHAPTER 3   RETURN ON INVESTMENT: Evaluating Education, Work, and Business

For the following problems, figure the return on investment.

	End-of-Period Wealth	Beginning-of-Period Wealth	ROI in %
6.	$25	$ 20	_____
7.	200	100	_____
8.	60	20	_____
9.	250	500	_____

10. _____ means the chance of losing your investment.

OPPORTUNITY RECOGNITION

CRITICAL THINKING ABOUT... RECOGNIZING OPPORTUNITIES

1. Explain how a business opportunity differs from a business idea.

2. Give an example of a change that has occurred or is about to occur in your neighborhood. Discuss any business opportunities this change might create.

3. Do you have artistic ability? How might you turn your talent into a business?

4. List your hobbies, skills, resources, and interests, and those of a friend. Describe three businesses you or he/she could start alone or together.

CHAPTER 4   OPPORTUNITY RECOGNITION

5. Choose a business you would like to start, and perform a SWOT analysis.

   Type of Business: _____

   Strengths (Entrepreneur's abilities and contacts)
   _____
   _____
   _____

   Weaknesses (The problems the entrepreneur faces, from lack of money or training to lack of time or experience.)
   _____
   _____
   _____

   Opportunities (Lucky breaks or creative advantages the entrepreneur can use to get ahead of the competition.)
   _____
   _____
   _____

   Threats (Anything that might be bad for the business, from competitors to legal problems.)
   _____
   _____
   _____

6. Do you have a part-time job or do you work around the house to earn money? Describe how you could apply entrepreneurial thinking to your work to earn more money.
   _____
   _____
   _____
   _____
   _____

MODULE 1 UNIT 1

KEY CONCEPTS

Given these hypothetical situations, which business would you consider starting or investing in?

1. A 100% increase in the price of gasoline.

2. A going-out-of-business sign in the window of a local grocery store.

3. A new airport being built near your home.

4. An increase in the percentage of women entering the workforce.

5. Local government decides to privatize garbage collection and impose recycling on households.

6. The state government allows parents to receive a sum of money that they can spend as they wish on education for their children.

CHAPTER 4 — OPPORTUNITY RECOGNITION

EXPLORATION

Have a conversation with a parent or other adult relative. Ask this person to tell you about which things he or she finds frustrating in the neighborhood. Write down these complaints.

Step 1: Generate at least three business opportunities from this conversation.

Step 2: Evaluate each of these using the "Business Opportunities" questions below.

Step 3: Choose one of these business opportunities and write a SWOT analysis.

Opportunity 1: _____

Is it attractive to customers?	Yes	No
Will it work in your business environment?	Yes	No
Is there a reasonable window of opportunity?	Yes	No
Do you have the skills and resources to create this business?	Yes	No
If you do not have the skills and resources to create this business, do you know someone who does and might want to help bring it into existence?	Yes	No
Do you think you can supply the product or service at a price that will attract customers, yet earn a profit?	Yes	No

Opportunity 2: _____

Is it attractive to customers?	Yes	No
Will it work in your business environment?	Yes	No
Is there a reasonable window of opportunity?	Yes	No
Do you have the skills and resources to create this business?	Yes	No
If you do not have the skills and resources to create this business, do you know someone who does and might want to help bring it into existence?	Yes	No
Do you think you can supply the product or service at a price that will attract customers, yet earn a profit?	Yes	No

Opportunity 3: _____

Is it attractive to customers?	Yes	No
Will it work in your business environment?	Yes	No
Is there a reasonable window of opportunity?	Yes	No
Do you have the skills and resources to create this business?	Yes	No
If you do not have the skills and resources to create this business, do you know someone who does and might want to help bring it into existence?	Yes	No
Do you think you can supply the product or service at a price that will attract customers, yet earn a profit?	Yes	No

MODULE 1   UNIT 1

SWOT ANALYSIS

Complete a SWOT analysis of one of the business opportunities you identified.

Type of Business: _____

Strengths (Entrepreneur's abilities and contacts)

_____
_____
_____

Weaknesses (The problems the entrepreneur faces, from lack of money or training to lack of time or experience.)

_____
_____
_____

Opportunities (Lucky breaks or creative advantages the entrepreneur can use to get ahead of the competition.)

_____
_____
_____

Threats (Anything that might be bad for the business, from competitors to legal problems.)

_____
_____
_____

IN YOUR OPINION

For each situation listed below, describe your greatest opportunity cost (that is, your next-best investment).

1. You spend $20 on a new shirt.

_____
_____
_____

CHAPTER 4 OPPORTUNITY RECOGNITION

2. You watch TV for five hours.
   _____
   _____
   _____

3. You invest $10 in your brother's lemonade stand at a guaranteed 100% ROI.
   _____
   _____
   _____

4. You put $10 in your savings account, where it will earn 3% interest.
   _____
   _____
   _____

VOCABULARY

benefits ■ cost/benefit analysis ■ opportunity ■ opportunity cost ■ SWOT analysis

1. If the _____ outweigh the costs, the investment will probably be worthwhile.

2. _____ is the cost of your next-best investment.

3. Before making any business or personal decision, perform a(n) _____ .

4. Perform a(n) _____ to evaluate a potential business opportunity or to evaluate a current business every few months.

5. A good idea can only become a(n) _____ if it is based on what consumers want.

MODULE 1   UNIT 1

CHAPTER 4 QUIZ
Opportunity Recognition

1. What does Albert Einstein's comment, "In the middle of difficulty lies opportunity" mean to you?

   _____
   _____
   _____

2. In the two scenarios below, write a sentence or two about how each problem could be viewed as an opportunity.

   After playing a sport in a nearby park, there was no place to get a drink.

   _____
   _____
   _____

   The arts and crafts supply store in your neighborhood closes and you and many of your friends depended on it.

   _____
   _____
   _____

3. You read a newspaper article that talks about the possibility of people being able to live on Mars someday. Would you consider this a business opportunity? Why or why not?

   _____
   _____
   _____
   _____
   _____
   _____

CHAPTER 4 OPPORTUNITY RECOGNITION

4. What are the five "roots of opportunity" in the marketplace?

   a. _____

   b. _____

   c. _____

   d. _____

   e. _____

5. List five ways (outside of your current interests) you could broaden the scope of your thinking.

   a. _____

   b. _____

   c. _____

   d. _____

   e. _____

6. Why is an idea not always an opportunity?

   _____

7. How long is a "window of opportunity" open?

   _____

MODULE 1   UNIT 1

8. What was the concept that Russell Simmons used to his advantage?

9. What are the eight basics of building a successful business?

   a.
   b.
   c.
   d.
   e.
   f.
   g.
   h.

10. What would be a way to keep track of ideas that identify business opportunities?

11. Explain "opportunity cost."

28

CHAPTER 5
CHARACTERISTICS OF THE SUCCESSFUL ENTREPRENEUR

CRITICAL THINKING ABOUT... CHARACTERISTICS OF AN ENTREPRENEUR

1. Take the NFTE "characteristics" survey below.

   HOW MUCH OF AN ENTREPRENEUR ARE YOU?

Quality	Explanation	Range
Drive	Highly motivated	1 2 3 4 5 6 7 8 9 10
Perseverance	Sticking to task or goal	1 2 3 4 5 6 7 8 9 10
Risk-Taking	Willing to take chances	1 2 3 4 5 6 7 8 9 10
Organization	Life and work in order	1 2 3 4 5 6 7 8 9 10
Confidence	Sure of yourself	1 2 3 4 5 6 7 8 9 10
Persuasiveness	Able to convince others	1 2 3 4 5 6 7 8 9 10
Honesty	Open, truthful	1 2 3 4 5 6 7 8 9 10
Competitiveness	Eager to win	1 2 3 4 5 6 7 8 9 10
Adaptability	Coping with new situations	1 2 3 4 5 6 7 8 9 10
Understanding	Empathy with others	1 2 3 4 5 6 7 8 9 10
Discipline	Self-control	1 2 3 4 5 6 7 8 9 10
Vision	Able to keep goals in mind	1 2 3 4 5 6 7 8 9 10

   (low ⟵⟶ high)

   Date _____   Total Score _____

2. What are your three strongest characteristics? What are your three weakest? How could you strengthen them?

   _____
   _____
   _____
   _____
   _____

CHAPTER 5   CHARACTERISTICS OF THE SUCCESSFUL ENTREPRENEUR

3. What does it mean to have self-esteem? Describe your self-esteem.

4. What kind of attitude is most important for the entrepreneur and why?

5. What are three things you could do to make your dreams come true? Write an essay about a time you successfully used any of these techniques to fulfill a goal.

KEY CONCEPTS

1. Do you agree or disagree with Napoleon Hill's statement about adversity, failure, and heartache? Explain.

MODULE 1   UNIT 1

2. Describe three core beliefs you would use to run your own company.

   _____
   _____
   _____

3. Write about a time you wanted to accomplish something, but couldn't. What would you do differently in that same situation today? Explain.

   _____
   _____
   _____

4. Describe three ways you could change to develop a more positive mental attitude.

   _____
   _____
   _____

5. Choose a positive saying or quotation as your personal motto. Write it on a sign using magic markers, spray paint, glitter, or other materials.

   _____
   _____
   _____

EXPLORATION

1. Collect at least three positive quotes or sayings from your parents or other adults. Share them with the class.

   _____
   _____
   _____

2. Discuss with a partner: *What is your attitude about money?*

   _____
   _____
   _____

CHAPTER 5   CHARACTERISTICS OF THE SUCCESSFUL ENTREPRENEUR

Does money solve problems? How important is it?

_____
_____
_____

Tell the class what you've learned about your partner's attitude toward money and how it differs from yours.

3. One of the biggest problems in the United States is the fact that so many people are overweight and out of shape. Entrepreneurs are responding with all kinds of products and services. Give three examples and bring advertisements or samples to show the class.

_____
_____
_____

VOCABULARY

Answer the following questions with complete sentences using the vocabulary words.

core belief ▪ optimist ▪ self-esteem

1. Are you an optimist? Why or why not?

_____
_____
_____

2. Write about a time when you were tempted to give up on something but didn't, or about a time when you did quit. What difference can perseverance make?

_____
_____
_____

3. How does stress in your life affect your confidence and mental attitude?

_____
_____
_____

MODULE 1 UNIT 1

CHAPTER 5 QUIZ
Characteristics of the Successful Entrepreneur

Match the correct definition with the traits below by writing the letter next to the trait.

1. perseverance _____   a. courage

2. vision _____   b. not giving up

3. organization _____   c. sticking to goals

4. risk-taking _____   d. keeping order

5. Why do entrepreneurs need to be optimists?
   _____
   _____
   _____

6. Why is honesty important in business?
   _____
   _____
   _____

On the following lines, write the letters of five of the quotations below that deal with perseverance and positive thinking.

7. _____
8. _____
9. _____
10. _____
11. _____

   a. Courage is resistance to fear, mastery of fear — not absence of fear.

   b. The more you do of what you've done, the more you'll have of what you've got.

   c. You must do the thing you think you cannot do.

   d. Our greatest glory is not in never falling down, but rising every time we fall.

CHAPTER 5 CHARACTERISTICS OF THE SUCCESSFUL ENTREPRENEUR

e. Keep away from people who try to belittle your ambition.

f. Nothing in the world can take the place of persistence.

g. The world turns aside to let any man pass who knows where he is going.

h. Success seems to be largely a matter of hanging on after others have let go.

i. Give a man a fish and you feed him for a day. Teach a man to fish and you feed him for a lifetime.

12. How did Clement Stone develop a positive mental attitude?

_____
_____
_____

13. What effects can fear and negative thinking have on the body?

_____
_____
_____

14. Explain the concept underlying this quote: "Who you decide you are determines who you will become," and how it relates to positive mental attitude.

_____
_____
_____
_____
_____
_____
_____
_____
_____
_____

SUPPLY AND DEMAND:
How Free Enterprise Works

CRITICAL THINKING ABOUT... SUPPLY AND DEMAND

1. Is there a product that you stop buying when its price goes up, even a little? Is there another product that you would keep buying even if its price rose considerably? Explain.

2. Choose a product you would like to sell. What factors would affect the demand for it? What factors would affect its supply?

3. In the two situations below, what signals are being sent to the business owners? Describe them in a brief essay on each.

   #1: You are a dairy and soybean farmer in Wisconsin. You spend half the time farming soybeans and the other half taking care of the cows. The price of milk has just gone up 50 cents a gallon. What signal is the market sending?

CHAPTER 6   SUPPLY AND DEMAND: How Free Enterprise Works

#2: You own a nightclub with a "1960s" theme that plays rock and roll from that decade. Your club has been very successful for the last few years, but lately it has not been full. People are going instead to the new club down the street that has a "1970s" theme and plays disco music. You've tried lowering the cover charge, but you are still losing money every night. What signal is the market sending you? What are some ways you could respond?

_____
_____
_____
_____
_____
_____
_____
_____

KEY CONCEPTS

1. What is likely to happen to the price of air conditioners in December? Why?

   _____
   _____
   _____

2. What would you expect to happen to the demand for gasoline if everyone began using electric cars?

   _____
   _____
   _____
   _____
   _____
   _____

MODULE 1   UNIT 1

3. How would you expect the use of electric cars to affect the availability of gasoline and its price?

___

4. Explain why a monopoly can charge any price for the products it sells. Can monopolies develop in a free market system? Why or why not?

___

5. After reading A Business for the Young Entrepreneur in your textbook, explain how Franklin is using the laws of suply and demand to make his business profitable.

___

EXPLORATION

Choose a product, such as a can of beans, that you know you can find in several different stores in your neighborhood. List the price in each store. Are the stores charging different prices? Why do you think that might be? What other factors, besides price, do you think might affect the supply or demand of a product?

___

CHAPTER 6   SUPPLY AND DEMAND: How Free Enterprise Works

VOCABULARY

Fill in the blanks with the correct vocabulary word.

capitalism ■ command economy ■ competition ■ demand ■ free enterprise system ■ market clearing price ■ monopoly ■ supply

1. Consumers communicate to business owners through their _____ for a product or service.

2. Business owners have to study the market to determine how much of a product to _____ .

3. The price at which quantity supplied equals quantity demanded is the _____ .

4. In a _____ the supplier doesn't have to compete to attract customers.

5. A _____ is an economy in which anyone is free to start a business. This type of economy is also called _____ .

6. In a _____ the government sets prices, and tells people where they can work and how much they can earn.

7. _____ encourages lower prices and higher quality.

MODULE 1   UNIT 1

CHAPTER 6 QUIZ

Supply and Demand: How Free Enterprise Works

1. Define "supply."

2. Define "demand."

3. Explain why you would or would not invest in an ice cream company that sold its products only in Alaska.

4. What is a "market clearing price"?

5. At a higher price, suppliers would want to sell _____ of a product.

6. At a lower price, consumers would want to buy _____ of a product.

CHAPTER 6 SUPPLY AND DEMAND: How Free Enterprise Works

7. Create a graph showing supply and demand. Mark the market clearing price on the graph.

[blank graph area]

8. If a shoe store has a great many unsold rain boots, what will eventually happen to the price?

_____
_____
_____

9. If electric cars replaced gasoline-powered cars, what would be the best business to have, of those below? (Circle one.)

   a. manufacturing batteries

   b. selling gasoline

   c. farming

INVENTIONS AND PRODUCT DEVELOPMENT

CRITICAL THINKING ABOUT... INVENTIONS

1. Prepare for the class Invention Contest by developing a new invention or a product improvement. Describe your invention briefly and include a drawing. Be sure to describe how your invention will meet a consumer need.

___
___
___
___
___
___
___
___

CHAPTER 7 INVENTIONS AND PRODUCT DEVELOPMENT

2. Choose an invention that you often use and research it on the Internet. Write a one-page report about the history of this invention.

3. Are you creative? Describe your creativity and come up with three ways you could become a more creative thinker.

4. For your own business, how do you plan to protect your business idea, product, or service: __ patent, __ copyright or __ trademark? Explain your choice.

KEY CONCEPTS

1. What is a prototype and why is it useful? How can you find a company to make a prototype of your invention?

2. Why can entrepreneurs be called the "artists" of the economy?

3. Do you have to be born with creativity or can you develop it? Explain.

MODULE 1   UNIT 2

IN YOUR OPINION

Discuss with a partner:

1. Write a list of businesses you could imagine starting. Ask your partner about his or her interests or hobbies. Now write a list of businesses you could imagine your partner starting, based on what you've learned. Compare and discuss your lists with your partner.

   _____
   _____
   _____
   _____
   _____
   _____
   _____
   _____

2. Think of a recording artist you and your partner both like. Discuss: Is this person a good entrepreneur? Is he or she setting or following trends? Is this artist aware enough of the market to stay on top? Report your findings to the class.

   _____
   _____
   _____
   _____
   _____
   _____

3. Would you go to the expense of making a prototype for a product that you invented? Why or why not?

   _____
   _____
   _____

4. Write a two-page report about the life of a minority or woman inventor. If you have access to the Internet, research the report online. If not, use library resources, such as an encyclopedia. (Use separate paper for this exercise.)

CHAPTER 7 INVENTIONS AND PRODUCT DEVELOPMENT

VOCABULARY

Choose the best definition from each set of answers. Circle your answers.

1. Creativity
    a. ability to be imaginative and inventive
    b. ability to imitate
    c. ability to think vertically

2. Lateral thinking
    a. thought that stacks ideas
    b. thought that challenges assumptions and provokes new ideas
    c. thought that develops "concept prisons"

3. Vertical thinking
    a. creative way of thinking
    b. thought that discourages "concept prisons"
    c. thought that stacks ideas

4. Prototype
    a. a rough product model
    b. an exact product model
    c. a type of product

5. Invention
    a. a rough product model
    b. a new creation that can be used for a practical purpose
    c. a type of product

6. Patent
    a. a type of invention
    b. a model of an invention
    c. the exclusive right to produce, use, and sell an invention

MODULE 1   UNIT 2

CHAPTER 7 QUIZ
Inventions and Product Development

1. Explain why you agree or disagree with the quotation, "When you cease to dream, you cease to live."

   _____
   _____
   _____

2. What is a patent?

   _____
   _____
   _____

3. Pick an invention discussed in class or the text and describe how the inventor came up with the idea for it.

   _____
   _____
   _____

List three inventions and the needs they filled.

Invention	Consumer Need Filled
4.	
5.	
6.	

CHAPTER 7   INVENTIONS AND PRODUCT DEVELOPMENT

7. List another invention and give the inventor's name.
   _____
   _____
   _____

8. If an invention is in general use without a patent for one year, what can happen?
   _____
   _____
   _____

9. How is a patent registered?
   _____
   _____
   _____

10. List three ways to improve your creativity.
    _____
    _____
    _____

SELECTING YOUR BUSINESS:
What's Your Competitive Advantage?

CRITICAL THINKING ABOUT... SELECTING YOUR BUSINESS

1. List your hobbies, interests, and skills.

2. Think of five businesses you could start using your unique knowledge and your hobbies, interests, and skills. Choose a type for each business — retail, wholesale, service, or manufacturing.

3. Choose one of your business ideas and come up with a name. Explain the reasoning behind your choice.

CHAPTER 8   SELECTING YOUR BUSINESS: What's Your Competitive Advantage?

4. Describe the people who will make up the market for the business you have chosen.
   _____
   _____
   _____

5. What is your competitive advantage?
   _____
   _____
   _____
   _____

KEY CONCEPTS

1. List five ideas for businesses you would be interested in starting. Discuss them with a partner. Ask him/her to help you evaluate your ideas by asking questions like:
   - Does the idea satisfy a consumer need?
   - Do you have the skills and resources to create this business?
   - What would be your competitive advantage?

   Switch roles and help your partner evaluate his or her ideas. At the end of the discussion, you should each have chosen one business idea to pursue.
   _____
   _____
   _____
   _____
   _____

2. Write about your business idea. Describe it, and explain how you came up with it. Why do you think your idea will be a success?
   _____
   _____
   _____
   _____
   _____

MODULE 1   UNIT 2

3. Read A Business for the Young Entrepreneur on page 115 of the textbook. Write a mission statement for Andre's business.

   _____
   _____
   _____
   _____
   _____
   _____
   _____

EXPLORATION

1. Research one of the foundations listed in this chapter on the Internet and write a one-page report describing who started the foundation, what it does, and how it makes the world a better place. (Use separate paper for this exercise.)

2. Describe how you plan to pay yourself when you start your own business. Why did you choose this method?

   _____
   _____
   _____
   _____
   _____

VOCABULARY

Answer the following questions with complete sentences using the vocabulary words.

competitive advantage ■ foundation ■ manufacturing ■ philanthropy ■ product ■ retail ■ service ■ wholesale

1. What is the main difference between a product and a service?

   _____
   _____
   _____

CHAPTER 8   SELECTING YOUR BUSINESS: What's Your Competitive Advantage?

2. Is your business idea based on a product or service? Why?

   _____
   _____
   _____
   _____
   _____
   _____

3. What is the competitive advantage of your business idea?

   _____
   _____
   _____
   _____
   _____
   _____

4. What are the four types of businesses? How are they different?

   _____
   _____
   _____
   _____
   _____
   _____

5. What is the connection between philanthropy and entrepreneurship?

   _____
   _____
   _____
   _____
   _____
   _____

MODULE 1   UNIT 2

CHAPTER 8 QUIZ
Selecting Your Business: What's Your Competitive Advantage?

1. Do you agree that it is a good idea to start a "simple" business? Explain.

2. List five realistic business ideas you would seriously consider.

    a.

    b.

    c.

    d.

    e.

3. What should you remember in choosing a name for your business?

4. What benefits can result from turning a hobby into a business?

CHAPTER 8   SELECTING YOUR BUSINESS: What's Your Competitive Advantage?

5. For the following helpful hobbies or skills, write a corresponding suggestion for a business idea.

   Helpful Hobby/Skills   **Business Suggestions**

   a. Likes decorating for parties   _____
   b. Enjoys typing and proofreading   _____
   c. Speaks a second language   _____
   d. Loves animals   _____

6. Define "competitive advantage."
   _____
   _____
   _____

7. Pick three businesses you go to as a customer and describe their competitive advantages.

   a. _____
   _____
   _____
   _____
   _____

   b. _____
   _____
   _____
   _____
   _____

   c. _____
   _____
   _____
   _____
   _____

COSTS OF RUNNING A BUSINESS:
Variable and Fixed

CRITICAL THINKING ABOUT... COSTS OF RUNNING A BUSINESS

For the business below, define the unit of sale and create an EOU to determine the gross profit per unit.

Dave opens a retail jewelry store with an $80,000 start-up investment. On average, he sells $1,000 worth of jewelry per day to 50 customers. On average his cost of goods sold per customer is $5. His fixed monthly costs are:

Utilities	=	$250
Salary	=	$2,500
Advertising	=	$1,000
Interest	=	$0
Insurance	=	$1,000
Rent	=	$1,000
Depreciation	=	$500

a. What is Dave's economics of one unit of sale?

_____

_____

b. What are his total fixed costs per month?

_____

_____

c. What are his total fixed costs annually?

_____

_____

d. What is his total gross profit daily?

_____

_____

53

CHAPTER 9 — COSTS OF RUNNING A BUSINESS: Variable and Fixed

KEY CONCEPTS

1. What is the purpose of depreciation? How would you depreciate a used truck that you bought for your business for $4,000 and expected to have to replace in four years?

   _____
   _____
   _____

2. For a business you would like to start, estimate what you think the fixed and variable costs would be. Choose a category for each from USAIIRD: Utilities, Salaries, Advertising, Interest, Insurance, Rent, and Depreciation.

   _____
   _____
   _____

3. Contact a supplier you would like to use for your business and find out how much you would have to buy before getting a volume discount rate. Be sure they know you are a business, not an "end user" (consumer).

   _____
   _____
   _____

VOCABULARY

Use the following vocabulary words and chapter terms to complete the crossword puzzle.

- cost of goods sold
- cost of services sold
- depreciation
- direct cost
- fixed costs
- gross profit
- gross profit per unit
- fixed operating costs
- overhead
- net profit
- variable costs
- cash reserve
- economies of scale
- volume
- USAIIRD

ACROSS

1. Three months of fixed costs kept on hand for emergencies
6. Informal term for fixed costs
7. Seven common fixed costs
10. Another name for fixed costs
11. Selling price minus COGS and other variable costs
12. Costs that change depending on how many sales you make
13. Costs that stay the same regardless of sales
14. COGS before the product is sold

DOWN

1. Costs associated specifically with each unit of sale
2. Advantages of business growth, e.g., better deals from suppliers
3. For a service business, the cost of selling one additional unit
4. The quantity of an item you buy or sell
5. Selling price per unit minus total variable costs per unit
8. A method of saving the money needed to replace expensive equipment
9. What is left over after you pay your fixed costs out of your gross profit

CHAPTER 9 QUIZ

Costs of Running a Business: Variable and Fixed

1. What is the difference between a variable and a fixed cost?

2. What are five fixed costs?

3. What is the cost of goods sold if Hector pays $5 per tie and sells four dozen?

4. What is subtracted from gross profit to get the net profit?

5. Hector has sold his ties for $10 each. He spent $10 on renting a table at a trade fair and $20 on flyers to advertise his business. Use the cost of goods sold in Question 3 to find Hector's profit.

MODULE 1   UNIT 2

6. Would a commission paid to a salesperson on each item of merchandise sold be a fixed or variable cost?

_____

_____

_____

7. If a sandwich sells for $5 and costs $2 to make, what is the gross profit?

_____

_____

_____

8. If 100 sandwiches are sold each day at $3 profit per sandwich, and the daily operating costs are $50, what is the profit on each?

_____

_____

_____

CHAPTER 10

WHAT IS MARKETING?

CRITICAL THINKING ABOUT... FINDING YOUR MARKET

1. Who is in your market?

2. Make a list of the groups below that you think are in your market and describe each in a few sentences.

- Friends

- Classmates

- Relatives

- Young children

CHAPTER 10 WHAT IS MARKETING?

- Adult women
  _____
  _____
  _____

- Adult men
  _____
  _____
  _____

- Elderly adults
  _____
  _____
  _____

- Local people
  _____
  _____
  _____

- Businesspeople
  _____
  _____
  _____

- Other
  _____
  _____
  _____
  _____
  _____
  _____

KEY CONCEPTS

1. What is the business you hope to start? What is the primary benefit you think will attract customers? In the mind of the potential customer, what need would be fulfilled by your product?

   _____
   _____
   _____
   _____
   _____
   _____
   _____
   _____
   _____
   _____

2. Describe "The Four P's" in detail as they apply to your business idea.

   _____
   _____
   _____
   _____
   _____
   _____
   _____
   _____
   _____
   _____
   _____

CHAPTER 10 WHAT IS MARKETING?

3. Using the chart on page 114, fill out a marketing plan for your business.

EXPLORATION

1. Create a logo for your business, either by drawing it on a piece of paper, or with computer software.

2. Create an advertising flyer for your business that includes its logo. Use computer software or design the flyer by hand on a separate piece of paper.

VOCABULARY

Fill in the blanks with the correct vocabulary word.

brand ▪ business card ▪ cause-related marketing ▪ logo ▪ marketing ▪ market share ▪ mind share ▪ publicity

1. _____ is free advertising obtained by getting your business mentioned in the media.

2. Identifying the consumer benefits of your product is the first step toward _____ it.

3. Always carry your _____ to give to potential customers and contacts.

4. Your _____ is a distinctive trademark or sign that represents your business.

5. The key to building a successful _____ is to focus it tightly on the one benefit you want customers to associate with your business.

6. Advertising builds awareness and _____ .

7. _____ is expressed as a percentage.

8. _____ is inspired by a commitment to a social, environmental, or political cause.

MODULE 1 UNIT 2

CHAPTER 10 QUIZ
What Is Marketing?

1. What is the difference between a product feature and a product benefit? Give an example of a product feature and its benefit.

2. What does a brand do?

3. List five things you can do to build your brand.

4. List the "Four P's" of marketing.

5. Why is the location of a business important?

CHAPTER 10 WHAT IS MARKETING?

6. Why is "promotion" important?

_____
_____
_____

7. Why should you use business cards? To which "P" do they belong?

_____
_____
_____

8. What is the difference between mind share and market share?

_____
_____
_____

9. What are ways to include "giving back" in your marketing?

_____
_____
_____
_____
_____

10. What does the following quote mean? "If you tell lies about a product, you will be found out — either by the government, which will prosecute you, or by the consumer, who will punish you by not buying your product a second time."

_____
_____
_____
_____
_____
_____

CHAPTER 11

MARKET RESEARCH

CRITICAL THINKING ABOUT... MARKET RESEARCH

1. What is your target market? List three things you've found out about it.

   _____
   _____
   _____

2. Describe your market segment.

   - Choose five people from your market segment to research with a survey. Will you ask them questions face to face or give them a survey that they can complete anonymously? Why? What type of market research is this called? What are population statistics called?

   _____
   _____
   _____
   _____
   _____

   - Research your industry and display the results in a one-page report that includes pie charts and bar or line graphs. (Use separate paper for this exercise.)

3. Write ten questions for your market research survey. Ask the survey participants to respond to questions on a scale of one to four, or design your own range. Also ask five open-ended questions (questions that don't have a yes-or-no answer).

   Sample Survey Questions: (*1: not at all; 2: a little; 3: somewhat; 4: very much*)

1.	Do you like the name of my business?	1	2	3	4
2.	Would you buy my product?	1	2	3	4
3.	Do you think my product's price is fair?	1	2	3	4
4.	Do you prefer my product to that offered by my competitor?	1	2	3	4

CHAPTER 11 MARKET RESEARCH

Sample Open-Ended Survey Questions

1. How would you improve my business idea?
2. Where else would you go to buy my product?
3. What price do you think I should charge?

Your Survey Questions:

1. _____
2. _____
3. _____
4. _____
5. _____
6. _____
7. _____
8. _____
9. _____
10. _____

KEY CONCEPTS

1. How can market research prevent expensive mistakes?
   _____
   _____
   _____

2. What four factors should market research include, and why?
   _____
   _____
   _____
   _____

a. What type of statistics do you want to collect as market research for your business? Explain.

_____

_____

_____

b. What's the smartest thing you can do when a customer who bought your product or service says he or she did not like it?

_____

_____

_____

EXPLORATION

1. Have you found out who else offers your product/service in your area? Create a chart listing the names and:

   a. the prices they charge,

   b. the quality of the product or service (this could include customer complaints or features they really like),

   c. the quality of customer service.

Competition

Name of Company	Product/ Service	Price	Quality of Product/ Service	Quality of Customer Service
1.				
2.				
3.				
4.				
5.				

CHAPTER 11 MARKET RESEARCH

2. Write a brief essay explaining why your product/service is going to outperform the competition.

   Example: My DJ service is going to outperform the competition because my DJs always arrive 20 minutes early, in order to have time to get set up. They are also going to have a wider selection of music than my competitors, including lots of hip-hop, which our customers want to hear.

   _____
   _____
   _____
   _____
   _____
   _____
   _____
   _____
   _____
   _____
   _____
   _____
   _____
   _____

3. Would you consider getting a job with one of your competitors? Do you think this would be ethical? Why or why not?

   _____
   _____
   _____
   _____
   _____
   _____
   _____
   _____

MODULE 1 UNIT 2

VOCABULARY

Choose the best definition from each set of answers. Circle your answers.

1. Demographics
    a. consumer surveys
    b. market research
    c. population information

2. Statistics
    a. facts presented numerically
    b. records of consumer data
    c. library research

3. Market research
    a. listening to customers
    b. finding out who customers are
    c. both of the above

4. Market segment
    a. market share
    b. consumers who have a similar response to certain marketing
    c. both of the above

5. Survey
    a. set of questions that you ask consumers about product use, shopping habits, etc.
    b. a type of market research
    c. both of the above

CHAPTER 11 MARKET RESEARCH

CHAPTER 11 QUIZ
Market Research

Match the terms and definitions below.

1. _____ Statistics   a. a way of collecting information by asking questions of a sampling of people

2. _____ Surveys   b. numerical facts about particular groups of people

3. _____ Demographics   c. numerical facts of many kinds

4. What is the purpose of market research?
   _____
   _____
   _____

List three questions an automobile company might ask before mass-producing a new model car.

5. _____

6. _____

7. _____

8. What would you need to find out before opening a sporting goods store?
   _____
   _____
   _____

9. What general types of information do market researchers gather about people?
   _____
   _____
   _____

10. Name a product and then at least one question you would ask in a market research survey.
    _____
    _____

CHAPTER 12

KEEPING GOOD RECORDS

CRITICAL THINKING ABOUT... KEEPING GOOD RECORDS

1. Use the following transactions to complete the NFTE Journal pages on pages 72-75.

   Transaction

   4/1: You and a friend start a babysitter-training business by each investing $400 to sell two-hour sessions for $50 per session.

   4/2: You buy some computer equipment from PC Zone for $600 because you plan to deliver the training over a Web site; you write a purchase order.

   4/3: You hire another friend to help sell training sessions on 10% commission, to be paid at the end of every month.

   4/4: You print and distribute $100 worth of flyers and e-mails to young people to publicize your new business.

   4/6: Two people sign up for your training on purchase order.

   4/7: You invoice the two customers who signed up.

   4/8: An invoice comes from PC Zone for your computer equipment and you pay half of it on a two-payment installment plan.

   4/10: Your salesman friend brings you a check for 15 customers to take your training.

   4/11: You buy 50 certificates at $1 each to send to customers who complete your training.

   4/15: You receive a check for $50 from one of the customers you invoiced.

   4/17: You receive a check for $50 from one of the customers you invoiced.

   4/25: Three more people sign up, pay for and take your training.

   4/26: You pay your electricity bill for $16.

   4/27: You pay your Internet service provider monthly fee of $50.

   4/30: You pay 60 cents in postage for mailing a certificate to each customer who took your training this month.

   4/30: You calculate and write a commission check to your salesman.

   4/30: You determine your monthly profit.

   4/30: You pay 25% tax on your profit.

   4/30: You determine your after-tax profit.

NFTE Journal - 10 ©

Company: _____
Student Name: _____
Class / Section: _____
Teacher: _____

Month / Year: _____

(hint: Write the month and year large so it's easy to see.)

Cash is an ASSET

BALANCE FORWARD ↩

Ck No.	DATE	TO / FROM	FOR – With Number Details	DEPOSIT $ IN	PAYMENT $ OUT	BALANCE FORWARD
						-
1						
2						
3						
4						
5						
6						
7						
8						
9						
10						
11						
12						
13						
14						
15						
16						
17						
18						
19						
20						
21						
22						
23						
24						
25						
26						
27						
28						
29						
30						

1- If sales tax is collected in addition to selling price, it should be included in REVENUE. Sales tax will be calculated by multiplying REVENUE times the imputed sales tax rate for your State.
2- Only income taxes (on profit) are included on this line. Other taxes are included as business expenses.
3- Taxes owed, but not yet paid should be included in the total of Short-term Liabilities. When they are paid, Short-term Liabilities should be reduced by the amount paid.
4- Cost of Goods Sold (COGS) is the same as Cost of Services Sold (COSS) for a service business. Money spent on direct labor and materials (INVENTORY) is not a "cost" until it's sold, when it becomes COGS.
5- SALES is a synonym for (means the same thing as) REVENUE.
6- The dash symbol " - " stands for " 0 " (zero) in Accounting.

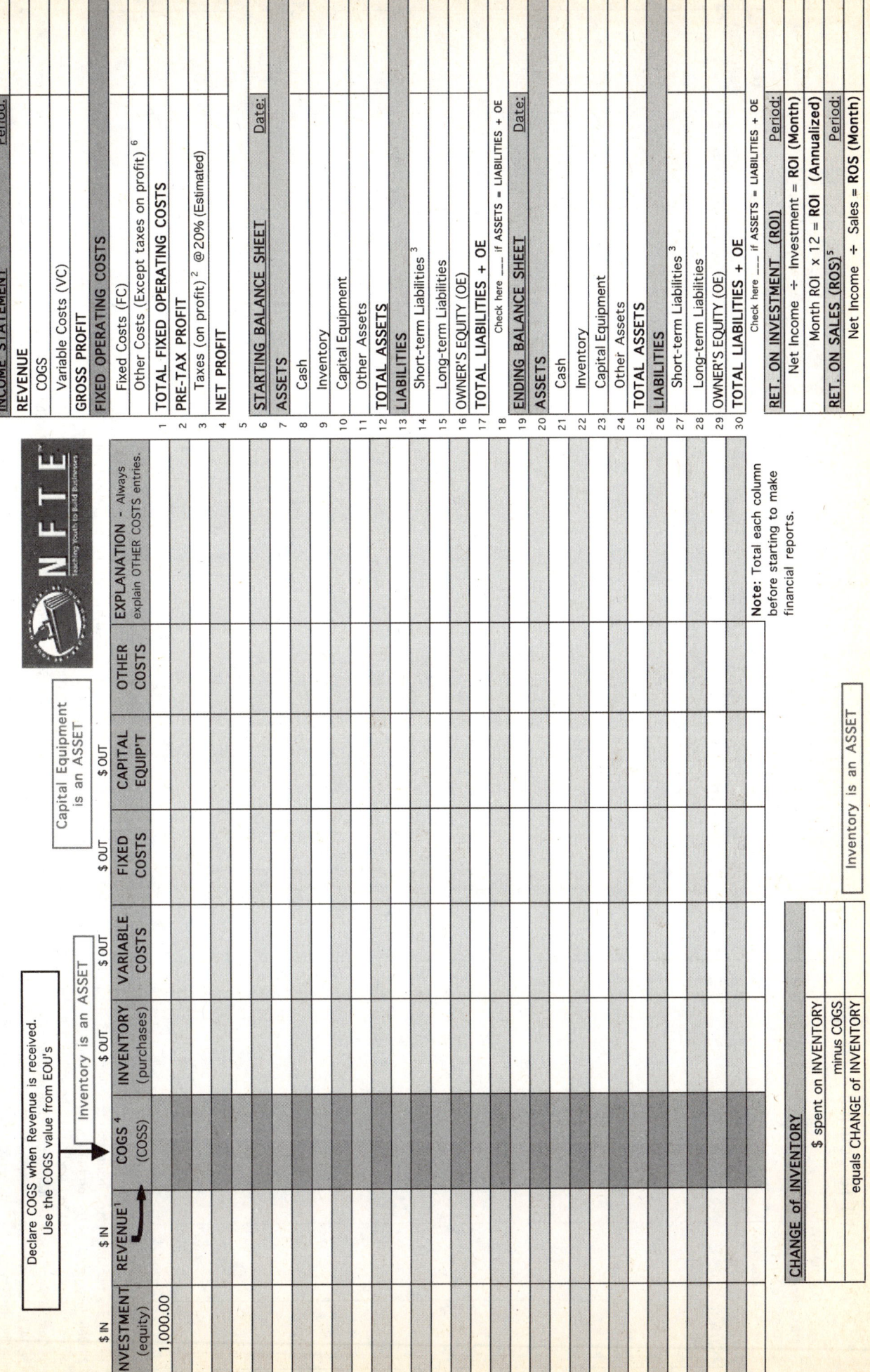

NFTE Journal - 10 ©

Company:
Student Name:
Class / Section:
Teacher:

Month / Year:

(hint: Write the month and year large so it's easy to see.)

Cash is an ASSET

Ck No.	DATE	TO / FROM	FOR - With Number Details	DEPOSIT $ IN	PAYMENT $ OUT	BALANCE FORWARD
						-
1						
2						
3						
4						
5						
6						
7						
8						
9						
10						
11						
12						
13						
14						
15						
16						
17						
18						
19						
20						
21						
22						
23						
24						
25						
26						
27						
28						
29						
30						

1- If sales tax is collected in addition to selling price, it should be included in REVENUE. Sales tax will be calculated by multiplying REVENUE times the imputed sales tax rate for your State.
2- Only income taxes (on profit) are included on this line. Other taxes are included as business expenses.
3- Taxes owed, but not yet paid should be included in the total of Short-term Liabilities. When they are paid, Short-term Liabilities should be reduced by the amount paid.
4- Cost of Goods Sold (COGS) is the same as Cost of Services Sold (COSS) for a service business. Money spent on direct labor and materials (INVENTORY) is not a "cost" until it's sold, when it becomes COGS.
5- SALES is a synonym for (means the same thing as) REVENUE.
6- The dash symbol " - " stands for " 0 " (zero) in Accounting.

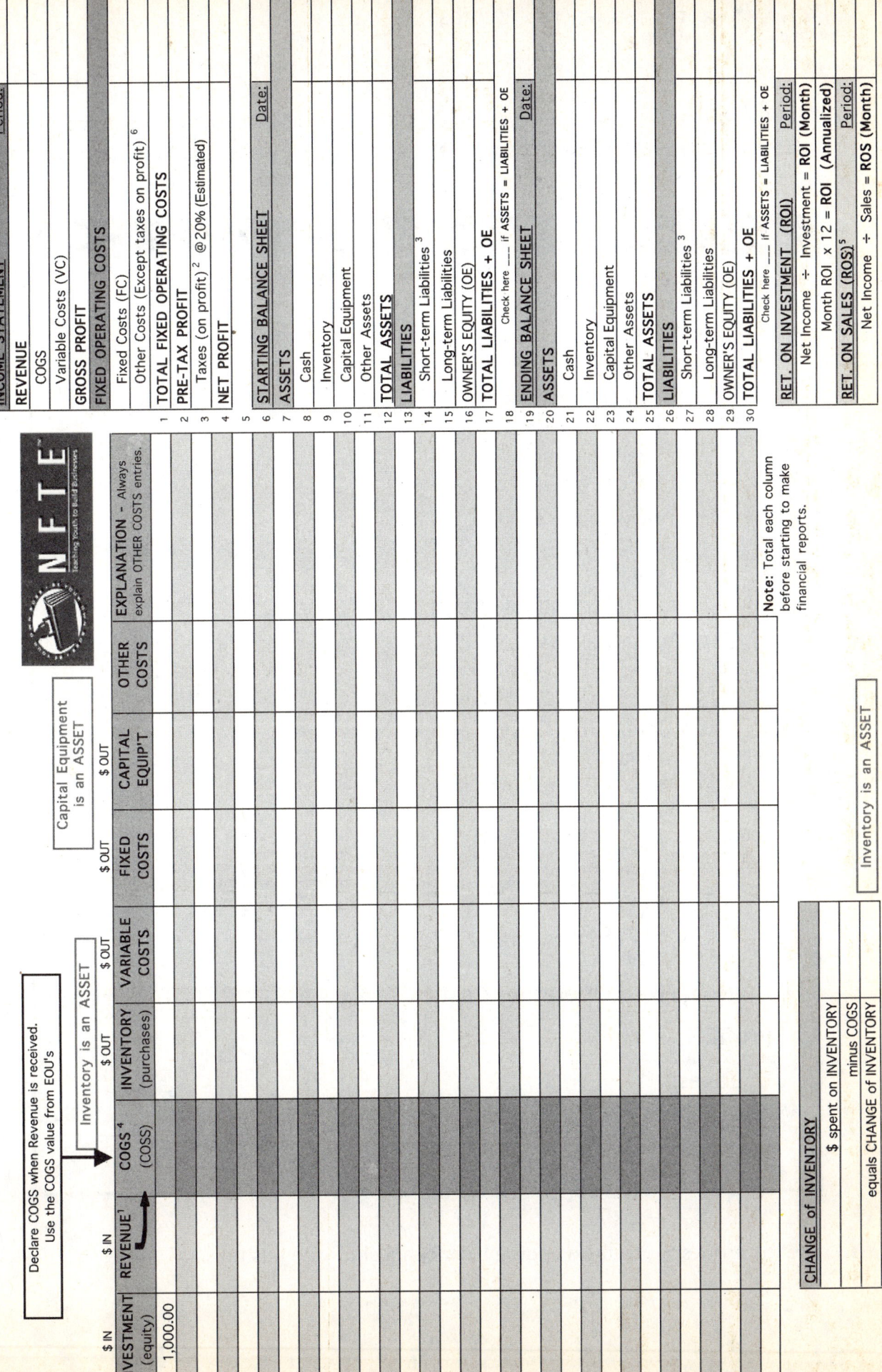

CHAPTER 12 KEEPING GOOD RECORDS

2. Use the entries to create an income statement for the business by writing down all your sales and subtracting all your costs. (In the next chapter, we will learn more about how to do an income statement.)

INCOME STATEMENT

Name of Company: _____   **Time Period:** _____

Sales/Revenue: $ _____

   Variable Costs

      Cost of Goods Sold

         Total Labor/Wage Costs: $ _____

         Total Supplies: _____

      Total Cost of Goods Sold: $ _____

      Other Variable Costs

         Commission: $ _____

         Shipping: _____

      Total Other Variable Costs: $ _____

   Total Variable Costs: $ _____   _____

Gross Profit: $ _____

   Fixed Operating Costs

      Utilities: $ _____

      Salary: _____

      Advertising: _____

      Insurance: _____

      Interest: _____

      Rent: _____

      Depreciation: _____

      Other: _____

   Total Fixed Operating Costs: $ _____

Profit: $ _____

   Taxes: _____

Net Profit: $ _____

3. Use the entries to create an ending balance sheet for the business.

MODULE 1 UNIT 3

BALANCE SHEET

Name of Company: _____   Time Period: _____

Assets
- Cash: $ _____
- Inventory: _____
- Capital Equipment: _____
- Other Assets: _____

Total Assets: $ _____

Liabilities
- Short-Term Liabilities: $ _____
- Long-Term Liabilities: _____

Owner's Equity: $ _____

Total Liabilities + OE: $ _____

4. Using the Journal you created, calculate the return on sales (ROS).

   _____
   _____
   _____

5. Using the Journal information, calculate the business's monthly and annual ROI.

   _____
   _____
   _____

KEY CONCEPTS

1. What bank accounts do you intend to set up? What bank will you be using?

   _____
   _____
   _____

2. Are banks required by law to offer all consumers the same rates and balance requirements? Explain.

   _____
   _____
   _____

CHAPTER 12 KEEPING GOOD RECORDS

3. Describe three reasons why it makes more sense to use checks instead of cash when running a business.
   _____
   _____
   _____

4. Describe the record-keeping system you intend to set up for your business.
   _____
   _____
   _____

IN YOUR OPINION

Discuss with a partner: Why do you think John D. Rockefeller kept track of every penny he spent? Do you think that was wise? Do you think it was possible? Write a brief essay and present your opinions to the class.

EXPLORATION

Visit three banks in your neighborhood and collect information about the checking and savings accounts they offer. Write a memo explaining which bank you are going to choose for your accounts.

CHAPTER 12 KEEPING GOOD RECORDS

VOCABULARY

Match the vocabulary word to its correct definition.

a. audit
b. deduction
c. invoice
d. packing slip
e. purchase order
f. receipt
g. taxes
h. transaction

1. _____ a receipt contained in a shipment you receive
2. _____ the percentage of your income paid to the government
3. _____ a record of what you ordered, from whom, at what price, and who took your order
4. _____ a bill
5. _____ a record that includes the date, what was purchased, and how much was paid
6. _____ a payment or deposit
7. _____ a visit from the Internal Revenue Service to check a business's financial records
8. _____ an expense that can legally be subtracted from taxes

CHAPTER 12 QUIZ

Keeping Good Records

1. What is the importance of keeping good records?

2. Do you think that John D. Rockefeller's habit of keeping track of every penny he spent had anything to do with his success? Explain.

3. Why does the NFTE Journal require you to record each amount twice?

CHAPTER 12 KEEPING GOOD RECORDS

Record the following transactions on a separate sheet of paper in record-keeping form:

4. On April 1st, 2008 you receive $200 from your part time job. You decide to invest $150 of that in your business. After depositing your paycheck in your personal checking account (never mix personal and business money) you write a personal check for $100 to your business, Snack-N-Go.

5. On April 4th, you buy assorted snack foods from Costco to resell at the flea market. You pay $65.00 with Snack-N-Go check number 120.

6. On April 6th, you buy subway tokens for the month. You write check number 121 to the City of New York for $8.00.

7. Also on April 6th, you stop at the Corner Print Shop to buy business cards. Your check number 122 is for $16.00.

8. Finally on April 6th, you buy poster board and art supplies to decorate your table. Your check number 123, to Pearl Art Supply, is for $24.00.

9. On April 9th, you arrive at Super Flea Market and pay them $10.00 to register and get a table for the weekend. Your check is number 124.

10. On April 11th, you deposit the money you received from sales (revenue) in the Snack-N-Go checking account. You sold out everything and took in $225.00.

11. You paid for lunch "out of pocket" (with your own money) at the flea market. Since that's part of the cost of selling, it is a legitimate business expense. To reimburse yourself for those costs, you write check no. 125 to yourself out of the Snack-N-Go checkbook. At the same time you mark "paid" and the date, April 11th, on the receipts, which you save with your Snack-N-Go business records.

12. On April 12th, you're back at Costco to stock up on snacks for next weekend. This time the check is number 126 for $90.00.

13. On April 16th, you return to the flea market. Your check number 127 for $10.00 rents your table for the weekend.

14. On April 18th, you deposit $248.00 from sales in the Snack-N-Go checking account.

15. On the same day you write yourself a reimbursement check, number 128 for $22.00 to cover the lunches and snacks you paid for personally over the weekend.

CHAPTER 13

INCOME STATEMENTS:
The Entrepreneur's Scorecard

CRITICAL THINKING ABOUT... INCOME STATEMENTS

1. Suppose you have a business selling caps to friends and classmates. This month you bought 20 caps for $5 each and sold them all at $10 each. You paid $40 in commissions to your brother to help sell them, and you spent $20 on posters (FC) as advertising. Your taxes are 20% of your pre-tax profit. Prepare your income statement.

Name of Company:	Time Period:
Sales/Revenue:	$ _____
Variable Costs	
Cost of Goods Sold	
Total Labor/Wage Costs:	$ _____
Total Supplies:	_____
Total Cost of Goods Sold:	$ _____
Other Variable Costs	
Commission:	$ _____
Shipping:	_____
Total Other Variable Costs:	$ _____
Total Variable Costs:	$ _____
Gross Profit:	$ _____
Fixed Operating Costs	
Utilities:	$ _____
Salary:	_____
Advertising:	_____
Insurance:	_____
Interest:	_____
Rent:	_____
Depreciation:	_____
Other:	_____
Total Fixed Operating Costs:	$ _____
Profit:	$ _____
Taxes:	_____
Net Profit:	$ _____

CHAPTER 13 INCOME STATEMENTS: The Entrepreneur's Scorecard

2. After preparing the income statement for the cap business, answer these questions:

   a. What is the cost of goods sold (COGS)?

   _____
   _____
   _____

   b. What is the net profit?

   _____
   _____
   _____

   c. What is the difference between gross profit and profit before taxes?

   _____
   _____
   _____

   d. How much was paid in taxes?

   _____
   _____
   _____

3. Using the income statement for the cap business, prepare a same size analysis and a pie chart.

Income statement line items	Dollars	Math	% of sales
Sales			
Less Total COGS			
Less Variable Costs			
Gross Profit			
Less Fixed Operating Costs			
Profit			
Taxes			
Net Profit/(Loss)			

4. Let's say the cap business earns a net profit of $20 in January; in February, $40; in March, $50; in April, $30, and $60 in May. Show this as a bar graph. Write a brief memo forecasting sales for the business for the rest of the year and describe what purchasing and hiring decisions you would make if you were running the business.

_____
_____
_____
_____
_____
_____

5. Which cost does the wise entrepreneur always keep secret? Why?

_____
_____
_____

CHAPTER 13 INCOME STATEMENTS: The Entrepreneur's Scorecard

KEY CONCEPTS

Using the McDonald's one-year income statement below, answer these questions:

SAMPLE MCDONALD'S INCOME STATEMENT

McDonald's	Time Period: December 20--	
	1 Month	1 Year
Sales/Revenue:	$300,000	$3,600,000
Variable Costs		
Cost of Goods Sold		
Food:	$66,000	$792,000
Paper:	9,000	108,000
Total:	$75,000	$900,000
Gross Profit:	$225,000	$2,700,000
Less Fixed Operating Costs	175,000	2,000,000
Profit Before Taxes:	$50,000	$700,000
Taxes:	15,000	233,000
Net Profit/(Loss):	$35,000	$467,000

1. What would the profit before taxes be if the owner finds a paper supplier who only charges $100,000 for the year?
   _____
   _____
   _____

2. What would the profit margin for the year be in that case?
   _____
   _____
   _____

MODULE 1 UNIT 3

3. Suppose you wanted to raise profits by $5,000 a month. What would you do and why?
   _____
   _____
   _____

4. How much do you think the business could be sold for? Why?
   _____
   _____
   _____

5. Do you have a business? If so, compare your income statement with that of McDonald's.
   _____
   _____
   _____

VOCABULARY

budget ■ financial ratios ■ income statement ■ net profit ■ operating ratio ■ percentage ■ pre-tax profit ■ profit margin ■ return on sales (ROS) ■ same size analysis

1. An entrepreneur uses a monthly _____ to track the business's sales and costs.

2. The financial ratio created by dividing sales into net profit is _____ .

3. _____ is the business's profit or loss after taxes have been paid.

4. When you divide sales into one of your fixed costs you get a(n) _____ .

5. You can create _____ from your income statement that will help you analyze your business.

6. A pie chart is based on _____ .

7. _____ is used to calculate how much taxes the business owes.

8. Another name for return on sales is _____ .

9. A _____ can show how each item on an income statement is affecting the business's profit.

10. A financial plan is also called an _____ .

CHAPTER 13 INCOME STATEMENTS: The Entrepreneur's Scorecard

CHAPTER 13 QUIZ
Income Statements: The Entrepreneur's Scorecard

1. Why is an income statement also called a profit and loss statement?
   _____
   _____
   _____

2. Why is it important to prepare an income statement once a month?
   _____
   _____
   _____

3. Why shouldn't an entrepreneur reveal his or her "cost of goods sold"?
   _____
   _____
   _____

4. Create an income statement on a separate piece of paper. Use the following information:

   Anna sells 20 bottles of perfume at $10 each.

   She bought the perfume at $2 per bottle.

   Anna spends $20 every month on a table at the trade fair.

   Her taxes are $.15 on every dollar of profit.

CHAPTER 14

FINANCING STRATEGY:
Debt or Equity?

CRITICAL THINKING ABOUT... FINANCING

1. Which type of financing, debt or equity, would you prefer to use to start your own business? Or would you use a blend? Explain, discussing the advantages and disadvantages of each type.

DEBT VS. EQUITY

DEBT: *Loans, Bonds*	EQUITY: *Stocks*
Advantages	*Advantages*
1.	1.
2.	2.
3.	3.
Disadvantages	*Disadvantages*
1.	1.
2.	2.
3.	3.

2. Interest is calculated by multiplying the principal by the interest rate. If $1,200 is borrowed at ten percent to be paid back over one year, the interest on the loan is $1,200 × .10 = $120. Fill in the blanks for the following loans:

Loan	Interest Rate	Interest Due for 1 Year
$1,400	_____ %	$140
$1,000	5%	$ _____
$400	20%	$ _____
$ _____	10%	$10

89

CHAPTER 14 FINANCING STRATEGY: Debt or Equity?

KEY CONCEPTS

Answer the following questions to complete the chart below.

1. What are the estimated costs of the items you will need to start your business? List each item and its cost.

2. How do you plan to finance your business? List your sources of financing, identifying whether each is equity, debt, or a gift.

3. What is the maximum percentage of ownership in the business that you would be willing to give up to secure equity financing? Why?

4. If you receive debt financing, what is the maximum interest rate you would be willing to pay? Why?

5. What is your debt/equity ratio and your debt ratio in the scenario given below? On your own paper, write a memo discussing the pros and cons of the entrepreneur's position.

Item	Estimated Cost	Financing Source	% Ownership	Interest Rate
Computer	*$800*	*Equity investment by brother*	*20%*	*n/a*
Inventory	*$1,600*	*Personal savings*	*100%*	*n/a*
Loan	*$3,200*	*Loan from family*	*0%*	*7%*

MODULE 1 UNIT 3

EXPLORATION: SHOPPING FOR A BANK

Visit three banks in your neighborhood and ask for information about their savings and checking accounts. Make a presentation to the class describing the costs and benefits of each bank's accounts. Explain which bank you will choose for your savings and which for checking.

	Costs	Benefits
Bank #1		
Bank #2		
Bank #3		

_____
_____
_____
_____
_____
_____

VOCABULARY

Use the following vocabulary words and chapter terms to complete the crossword puzzle on the following page.

- angel
- asset
- bankruptcy
- bootstrap financing
- cooperative
- corporation
- debt
- debt ratio
- debt-to-equity ratio
- equity
- financing
- leveraged
- nonprofit
- partnership
- payback
- promissory note
- sole proprietorship
- start-up capital

91

CHAPTER 14 FINANCING STRATEGY: Debt or Equity?

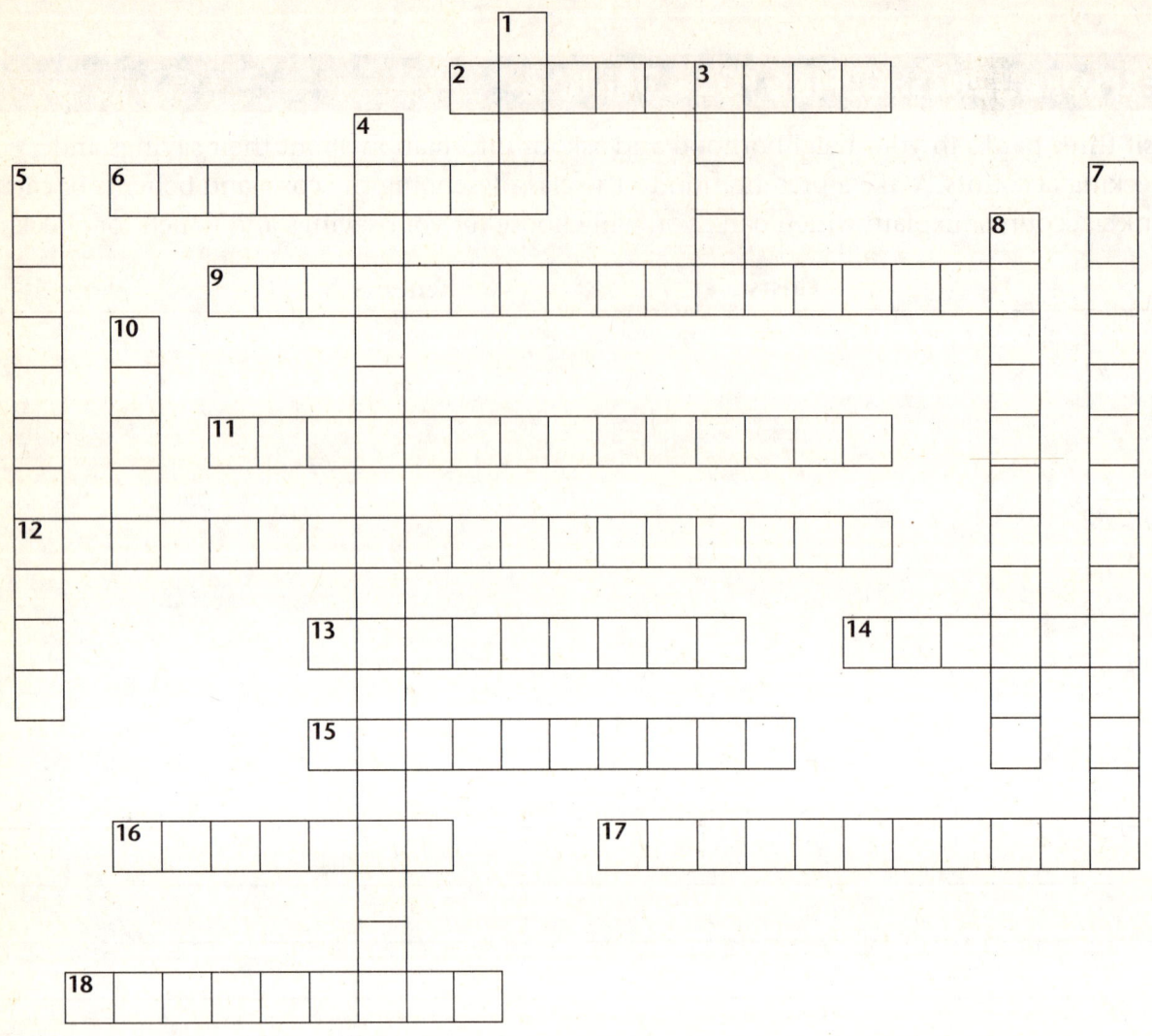

ACROSS

2 The ratio of debt to assets
6 A corporation whose mission is to improve society in some way
9 An expression of a company's financial strategy
11 One-time investment of starting a business
12 Business owned by one person
13 Raising capital for a business
14 To finance with this, the entrepreneur trades a percentage of ownership for money
15 When a lender goes to court to prove that a business owner cannot pay a debt
16 How long it will take your business to earn enough profit to cover the start-up investment
17 A business owned and controlled by the customer/members who use its services
18 Financed through debt

DOWN

1 To finance with this, the entrepreneur borrows money to be paid back with interest
3 Anything of value owned by a business
4 Strategy for getting a business off the ground with the lowest start-up costs possible
5 Business ownership shared by two or more people
7 If you borrow money from a bank, you will have to sign one of these
8 An entity composed of stockholders who own pieces of the company
10 A private investor who is worth over $1 million and is interested in backing start-up businesses

MODULE 1   UNIT 3

CHAPTER 14 QUIZ
Financing Strategy: Debt or Equity?

1. What are the advantages and disadvantages of opening a sole proprietorship or a partnership?

2. Explain equity financing.

3. Name an advantage of debt financing.

4. What is a disadvantage of debt financing?

5. Who would be taking a greater risk — a stock investor or a bond investor? Why?

6. Companies that get most of their financing from debt are described as (circle one).

    a. mortgaged

    b. leveraged

    c. having low assets

93

CHAPTER 14 FINANCING STRATEGY: Debt or Equity?

7. If a business sells $50,000 worth of stock and $100,000 in bonds, what is the debt-to-equity ratio?

8. If the assets of a company total $4 million and it has $1 million in debt, what would the debt ratio be?

9. Describe two types of alternative financing.

10. If Leticia opened a fashion earring business with $300 from her personal savings and a $200 loan from her parents, and she earns a monthly net profit of $50, how long would it take her to recover her investment?

CHAPTER 15

NEGOTIATION:
Achieving Goals through Compromise

CRITICAL THINKING ABOUT... NEGOTIATION

1. Play the Negotiating Game with your teacher's guidance. Write a short essay about how you did and how you might improve the next time you play.

2. Use negotiation strategies to get something you want, such as a later curfew, a favor from a friend, time off from work, etc. Write a paragraph describing your negotiation experience.

CHAPTER 15 NEGOTIATION: Achieving Goals through Compromise

KEY CONCEPTS

1. What is the difference between real negotiating and playing a game?

   _____
   _____
   _____
   _____

2. Why is it smart to seek a win/win conclusion to a negotiation?

   _____
   _____
   _____
   _____
   _____

3. Describe how you should get organized before a negotiation.

   _____
   _____
   _____
   _____
   _____

4. What should you always determine before entering a negotiation?

   _____
   _____
   _____
   _____
   _____

5. Describe three ways you can try to get the other person to reveal his or her position.

   _____
   _____
   _____
   _____
   _____

MODULE 1 UNIT 3

IN YOUR OPINION

Do you agree that negotiation is about compromise, not winning? Write a short essay giving your opinion and share it with classmates.

CHAPTER 15 NEGOTIATION: Achieving Goals through Compromise

VOCABULARY

Choose the best definition from each set of answers. Circle your answers.

1. Compromise

   a. failure to come to an agreement

   b. negotiation in which only one party is willing to bargain

   c. an agreement in which both parties have given up something

2. Negotiation

   a. achieving one's goals through give-and-take

   b. achieving all your own goals at the other person's expense

   c. winning an argument

MODULE 1 UNIT 3

CHAPTER 15 QUIZ
Negotiation: Achieving Goals through Compromise

1. What should you do before a negotiation?

2. Waiting for the other person to make the first offer, throwing out an extremely high (or low) figure, or keeping silent, are all ways to make him/her _____.

3. On her last sales call, Lourdes kept talking until the customer said "Maybe." Should Lourdes be content with that? What should she do?

4. By the end of the negotiations, Mike had gotten a much higher price than he expected. Also, he agreed to none of the conditions Barry wanted. Barry had finally agreed but was very unhappy. Was Mike successful? Explain.

Fill in the correct words for the two sentences below.

5. _____ is an agreement in which both parties give something up.

6. _____ is a process of trying to attain the goals of both parties through give and take.

CHAPTER 15 NEGOTIATION: Achieving Goals through Compromise

7. Malika would like to borrow money to start a jewelry business. The lender agrees, if the money can be paid back in ten days. What should Malika do next?

   _____
   _____
   _____

8. Hector is willing to buy two dozen ties at $2 each. The wholesaler wants to sell four dozen at $4 each. Suggest a reasonable compromise.

   _____
   _____
   _____

9. Why is it smart to seek a win/win result in a negotiation?

   _____
   _____
   _____

10. Below (or on a separate piece of paper), give an example of a negotiation in which both parties were satisfied.

    _____
    _____
    _____
    _____
    _____
    _____
    _____
    _____
    _____

CHAPTER 16

FROM THE WHOLESALER TO THE TRADE FAIR: *A Real-Life Business Experience*

CRITICAL THINKING ABOUT... SELLING AT A TRADE FAIR

1. Use your local *Business to Business* telephone directory to call two vendors of a product you would like to buy and resell. Get the following information from each:

   Vendor #1: Name _____

   Phone # _____

   Cost of One Unit _____ Minimum quantity that can be purchased _____

   Availability _____ Delivery time _____

   Vendor #2: Name _____

   Phone # _____

   Cost of One Unit _____ Minimum quantity that can be purchased _____

   Availability _____ Delivery time _____

2. After you have purchased inventory at a wholesaler for your trade fair field trip, write a short essay analyzing the experience. What did you buy? How much did you pay? How well do you think you negotiated?

   _____
   _____
   _____
   _____
   _____
   _____
   _____
   _____
   _____
   _____

CHAPTER 16 FROM THE WHOLESALER TO THE TRADE FAIR: A Real-Life Business Experience

3. Use your inventory and sales sheets to create an income statement after your trade fair (flea market) selling experience.

TRADE FAIR SALES (SAMPLE)

Product	A Units Sold (make mark for each sale)	×	B Wholesale Cost Per Unit	=	C Total Cost of Goods Sold	D Selling Price Per Unit	(A × D) Total Sales
_____	_____		_____		_____	_____	_____
_____	_____		_____		_____	_____	_____
_____	_____		_____		_____	_____	_____
_____	_____		_____		_____	_____	_____
							Totals

My Income Statement

My Total Sales are: $ _____

My Total Cost of Goods Sold is: $ _____

My Gross Profit is: $ _____

    My Operating Costs are:

        My Fixed Operating Costs are: $ _____

My Total Fixed Operating Costs are: $ _____ $ _____

My Net Profit/(Loss) is: $ _____

EXPLORATION

1. Call your local chamber of commerce and make a list of trade fairs and open markets in your area.

_____ _____
_____ _____
_____ _____

MODULE 1   UNIT 3

2. Use your local telephone company's *Business to Business Guide* or *The American Wholesalers and Distributors Directory* to locate wholesalers you could visit or from whom you could order products for resale. Make a list of them.

VOCABULARY

Choose the best definition from each set of answers. Circle your answers.

1. Inventory sheet
   a. an efficient way to keep track of goods and sales
   b. at-a-glance look at how much profit is being made on each sale
   c. record of markups on each item of inventory
   d. all of the above

2. Trade fair
   a. market where entrepreneurs own permanent retail space
   b. market where entrepreneurs rent space for a day or season
   c. market where consumers are looking for expensive luxury items
   d. all of the above

CHAPTER 16 QUIZ

From the Wholesaler to the Trade Fair: A Real-Life Business Experience

1. What are three things you will need to bring with you to a trade fair besides the merchandise you will be selling?
   _____
   _____
   _____

2. What should you give to a customer to verify the purchase?
   _____

3. How should you keep track of your money?
   _____

4. After the trade fair, you have the following cash on hand:

   50 pennies; 20 nickels; 20 quarters; 70 one dollar bills; 60 five dollar bills; 10 ten dollar bills; 4 twenty dollar bills

   What is your total cash? $ _____

5. You brought with you to the fair the following change:

   1 ten dollar bill; 10 five dollar bills; 10 one dollar bills; 20 quarters; 20 nickels; 50 pennies

   What is the total? $ _____

6. You have sales receipts for 80 belts at $5.50 each plus 50 cents sales tax. You have 15 unsold belts. What is the total of your receipts?
   _____

7. Does your cash on hand match your receipts? _____

8. You had an inventory of 100 belts with you at the start of the fair. Have you lost any?
   _____

9. If you paid $2 for each belt, what is the total cost of goods sold? $ _____

10. Assume you paid $10 for the table, gave away $5 worth of business cards and flyers, and your tax rate is 10%. Prepare an income statement on a separate piece of paper.

Basic Module
Business Plan Review

A business plan is the road map that gives a business direction.
— Joseph Mancuso, *author of How to Write a Winning Business Plan*

What Is a Business Plan?

A business plan is a document that explains a business idea and how it will be carried out. The plan should include all costs and a marketing plan. It should describe how it will be financed and what the earnings are expected to be.

The number one reason to write a business plan is to organize your thoughts *before* you start your business. Most of the entrepreneurs mentioned in this book wrote a business plan before they made a single sale. A well-written plan will guide you every step of the way as you develop your business. It can also help you raise money from investors.

Why Do You Need a Business Plan?

Bankers, and other potential investors, will refuse to see an entrepreneur who does not have a business plan. You may have a brilliant idea, but if it is not written out, people will be unlikely to invest in your business.

A well-written plan will show investors that you have carefully thought through what you intend to do to make your business profitable. The more explanation you offer investors about how their money will be used, the more willing they will be to invest. Your plan should be so thoughtful and well written that the only question it raises in an investor's mind is: "How much can I invest?"

Writing a Business Plan Will Save You Time and Money

As you work on your plan, you will also be figuring out how to make your business work. Before you serve your first customer, you will have answered every question you can. How much should you charge for your product or service? What exactly is your product or service? What is one unit? What are your costs? How are you going to market your product or service? How do you plan to sell it? Figuring all this out in advance will save you time and money.

If you start your business without a plan, these kinds of questions can overwhelm you. By the time you have completed the following pages, though, you will have answers — and you will have a road map for your own business! You will also be able to use these answers to create a PowerPoint presentation that will hit the high points of your business plan.

Give detailed answers to the following business plan review questions. Use separate paper if you need additional space for your answers.

BASIC MODULE: BUSINESS PLAN REVIEW

Your Business Idea (Chapter 1)

1. Describe your business idea.
   _____
   _____
   _____
   _____
   _____
   _____
   _____
   _____
   _____
   _____

2. What is the name of your business?
   _____
   _____

3. Explain how your idea will satisfy a consumer need.
   _____
   _____
   _____
   _____

4. Provide contact information for each owner.
   _____
   _____
   _____
   _____

BASIC MODULE: BUSINESS PLAN REVIEW

5. If there is more than one owner, describe how the business ownership will be shared.

Economics of One Unit (Chapter 2)

1. Do you intend to pay yourself a salary, wage, dividend, or commission? Explain.

2. What type of business are you starting?

3. Calculate the Economics of One Unit for your business.

ECONOMICS OF ONE UNIT (EOU)	
Manufacturing Business: unit =	
Selling Price per Unit:	$ _____
Labor Cost per Hour: $ _____	
No. of Hours per Unit: _____ $ _____	
Materials per Unit: _____	
Cost of Goods Sold per Unit: $ _____	_____
Gross Profit per Unit:	$ _____

BASIC MODULE: BUSINESS PLAN REVIEW

ECONOMICS OF ONE UNIT (EOU)

Wholesale Business: unit = _____

Selling Price per Unit:	$ _____
Cost of Goods Sold per Unit:	_____
Gross Profit per Unit:	$ _____

Retail Business: unit = _____

Selling Price per Unit:	$ _____
Cost of Goods Sold per Unit:	_____
Gross Profit per Unit:	$ _____

Service Business: unit = _____

Selling Price per Unit:		$ _____
Supplies per Unit:	$ _____	
Labor Costs per Hour:	_____	
Cost of Goods Sold per Unit:	$ _____	
Gross Profit per Unit:		$ _____

Return on Investment (Chapter 3)

Business Goals:

1. What is your short-term business goal (less than one year)? What do you plan to invest to achieve this goal? What is your expected ROI?

   _____
   _____
   _____
   _____

BASIC MODULE: BUSINESS PLAN REVIEW

2. What is your long-term business goal (from one to five years)? What do you plan to invest to achieve this goal? What is your expected ROI?

   _____
   _____
   _____
   _____

Personal Goals:

1. What is your career goal? What do you plan to invest to achieve this goal? What is your expected ROI?

   _____
   _____
   _____
   _____

2. How much education will you need for your career?

   _____
   _____
   _____
   _____

3. Have you tried to get a part-time job related to your chosen career?

   _____
   _____
   _____
   _____

Opportunity Recognition (Chapter 4)

1. What resources and skills do you (and the other owners of your business) have that will help make your business successful?

   _____
   _____

BASIC MODULE: BUSINESS PLAN REVIEW

2. Perform a SWOT analysis of your business.

   Type of Business: _____

   Strengths (Entrepreneur's abilities and contacts)

   _____
   _____
   _____

   Weaknesses (The problems the entrepreneur faces, from lack of money or training to lack of time or experience.)

   _____
   _____
   _____

   Opportunities (Lucky breaks or creative advantages the entrepreneur can use to get ahead of the competition.)

   _____
   _____
   _____

   Threats (Anything that might be bad for the business, from competitors to legal problems.)

   _____
   _____
   _____

BASIC MODULE: BUSINESS PLAN REVIEW

Core Beliefs (Chapter 5)

1. Describe three core beliefs you will use in running your company.

   _____
   _____
   _____
   _____
   _____
   _____

2. Choose a motto for your company. (You can select or adapt from the 50 positive quotes in Chapter 5, find one elsewhere, or make up your own.)

   _____
   _____
   _____
   _____

Supply and Demand (Chapter 6)

1. What factors will influence the demand for your product or service?

   _____
   _____
   _____
   _____

2. What factors will influence the supply for your product or service?

   _____
   _____
   _____
   _____

BASIC MODULE: BUSINESS PLAN REVIEW

Product Development (Chapter 7)

How do you plan to protect your product/trademark/logo? (Check one, and explain.)

_____ patent

_____ copyright

_____ trademark

Explain: _____

Competitive Advantage (Chapter 8)

1. What is your competitive advantage?

   _____
   _____
   _____
   _____

2. How will your business help others? List all organizations to which you plan to contribute. (Your contribution may be time, money, your product, or something else.)

   _____
   _____
   _____
   _____

Operating Costs (Chapter 9)

1. List and describe your monthly fixed costs.

   _____
   _____
   _____

2. List and describe your monthly variable costs.

   _____
   _____
   _____

BASIC MODULE: BUSINESS PLAN REVIEW

3. Re-calculate your economics of one unit, allocating as many variable costs as possible.

ECONOMICS OF ONE UNIT (EOU)		
_____ **Business:** unit = _____		
Selling Price per Unit:		$ _____
Supplies/Materials:	$ _____	
Labor:	_____	
Cost of Goods Sold per Unit:	$ _____	$ _____
Commission:	$ _____	
Packaging:	_____	
Total Other Variable Costs per Unit:	$ _____	_____
Total Variable Costs per Unit:		$ _____ _____
Gross Profit per Unit:		$ _____

4. Add a cash reserve that covers three months of fixed costs.

_____
_____
_____
_____

Marketing (Chapter 10)

1. Describe the Four P's for your business.

    Product — Why will your product meet a consumer need?

    Place — Where do you intend to sell your product?

    Price — What price do you plan to sell your product for, and why?

    Promotion — How do you plan to advertise and promote your product?

_____
_____
_____
_____

BASIC MODULE: BUSINESS PLAN REVIEW

2. Fill out a marketing plan for your business.

	Street Vending	Your Own Home	Door to Door	Flea Markets	School/ Community	Through local stores	Youth Clubs	Internet	Other
Business Cards									
Posters									
Flyers									
Phone Sales									
Sales Calls									
Brochures									
Mailings									
Newspaper/ Radio/TV									
Web site									
Other									

BASIC MODULE: BUSINESS PLAN REVIEW

3. Do you intend to publicize your philanthropy? Why or why not? If you do, explain how you will work your philanthropy into your marketing.

___

Market Research (Chapter 11)

1. Research your industry and display the results in a one-page report that includes pie charts and bar or line graphs. Describe your target market within the industry. Use separate paper for this exercise.

2. Describe your market segment and the results of your research on this market segment.

___

Record Keeping (Chapter 12)

1. Describe your record-keeping system.

___

2. List all bank accounts you will open for your business.

___

BASIC MODULE: BUSINESS PLAN REVIEW

Projected Income Statement (Chapter 13)

1. Complete a monthly projected budget and one-year income statement for your business.

	Jan	Feb	Mar	Apr	May	Jun	Jul	Aug	Sep	Oct	Nov	Dec	Total
Units Sold*													
Unit Selling Price*													
Sales/Revenue													
Total Cost of Goods Sold													
Total Other Variable Costs													
Total Variable Costs													
Gross Profit													
Total Fixed Costs													
Profit													

Less Taxes (25%)	Net Profit

* Units Sold and Unit Selling Price are not part of the Income Statement but when multiplied together give Total Sales/Revenue.

- Total Sales/Revenue = Units Sold × Unit Selling Price
- Total Cost of Goods or Services Sold = Units Sold × Cost of Goods or Services Sold per Unit
- Total Other Variable Costs = Units Sold × Other Variable Costs per Unit
- Total Variable Costs = Total Cost of Goods or Services Sold + Total Other Variable Costs
- Gross Profit = Total Sales − Total Variable Costs
- Total Fixed Costs = Total of USAIIRDO
- Profit/(Loss) = Gross Profit − Total Variable Costs
- Taxes = Profit × .25 (Estimated)
- Net Profit = Profit − Taxes

2. Use your projected one-year income statement to calculate:

Projected ROI for one year: _____ %; Projected ROS for one year: _____ %

Financing Strategy (Chapter 14)

1. What legal structure have you chosen for your business? Why?

   _____
   _____
   _____
   _____

2. List the cost of the items you will need to buy to start your business.

   _____
   _____
   _____
   _____

3. Add up the items to get your total start-up capital.

Item	Where will you buy this?	Cost
_____	_____	_____
_____	_____	_____
_____	_____	_____
_____	_____	_____
_____	_____	_____
_____	_____	_____

   Estimated Total Start-Up Costs: $ _____

4. Add a cash reserve of three months' fixed costs.

   _____
   _____
   _____
   _____

BASIC MODULE: BUSINESS PLAN REVIEW

5. List the sources of financing for your start-up capital. Identify whether each source is equity, debt, or a gift. Indicate the amount and type for each source.

Source	Equity	Debt	Gift
Personal savings:	_____	_____	_____
Relatives:	_____	_____	_____
Friends:	_____	_____	_____
Investors:	_____	_____	_____
Grants:	_____	_____	_____
Other:	_____	_____	_____
Subtotal:	_____	_____	_____

   Total Equity + Total Debt + Total Gift = Total Financing : _____

   If you use equity financing, what percentage of ownership will you give up?
   _____
   _____
   _____
   _____

   If you use debt financing, what is the maximum interest rate you will pay?
   _____
   _____
   _____
   _____

6. What is your debt ratio? What is your debt-to-equity ratio?
   _____
   _____
   _____
   _____

BASIC MODULE: BUSINESS PLAN REVIEW

7. What is your payback period? In other words, how long will it take you to earn enough profit to cover start-up capital?

   _____
   _____

Negotiation (Chapter 15)

Describe any suppliers with whom you will have to negotiate.

_____
_____
_____
_____
_____
_____

Buying Wholesale (Chapter 16)

1. Where will you purchase the products you plan to sell, or the products you plan to use to manufacture the products you will be selling?

Name of Supplier/Item	Price
_____	$ _____
_____	$ _____
_____	$ _____
_____	$ _____
_____	$ _____
_____	$ _____

2. Have you applied for a sales-tax ID number?

   _____
   _____
   _____

BASIC MODULE: BUSINESS PLAN REVIEW

Business Plan Notes

COMPETITIVE STRATEGY:
Define Your Business, Mission, and Tactics

CRITICAL THINKING ABOUT... COMPETITIVE STRATEGY

1. Describe the difference between strategy and tactics.

2. What is included in the definition of a business?

3. Why are these elements important?

4. What key concepts should a business's mission statement contain and why?

5. Write a mission statement for a business in your neighborhood that you have dealt with.

6. Can you think of three competitive advantages for your generation?

CHAPTER 17 COMPETITIVE STRATEGY: Define Your Business, Mission, and Tactics

7. Imagine you would like to start a business creating T-shirts and stickers for local bands to sell to their fans. Describe your strategy, mission statement, and tactics. Use separate paper if you need additional space.

   _____
   _____
   _____

8. Use the following charts to define your own business, analyze your competitive advantage, and determine your tactics.

Business Definition Question	Response
1. *The Offer:* What products and services will be sold by the business?	1.
2. *Target Market:* Which consumer segment will the business focus on?	2.
3. *Production Capability:* How will that offer be produced and delivered to those customers?	3.

Competitive Advantage Question	Competitive Difference (USP)
1. *The Offer:* What will be better or different about the products and services that will be sold by the business?	1.
2. *Target Market:* What customers should be the focus of the business, to make it as successful as possible?	2.
3. *Production and Delivery Capability:* What will be better or different about the way that offer is produced and delivered to those customers?	3.

Tactical Question	Issues	Solutions
1. *Sales Plan:* Where and how will you sell to your customers?	How to identify prospects and convert them to sales.	
2. *Market Communications:* How will you communicate with your customers and make them aware of your business offer?	How to make customers aware of your offer; how to attract them to the business.	
3. *Operating Plan:* How will you manage your internal operations?	How to make the business go, and determine who will perform the tasks.	
4. *Budget:* How do you plan to manage your revenues and expenses?	What are the sources of revenue? What are the items that have to be purchased?	

KEY CONCEPTS

1. In order to succeed, does a company need to sell a product or service more cheaply than the competition? Explain.

___

___

CHAPTER 17 COMPETITIVE STRATEGY: Define Your Business, Mission, and Tactics

2. Write an essay describing your business's competitive advantage. Discuss the strategy and tactics you intend to use.

___

3. Write a mission statement for your business.

___

MODULE 2 UNIT 4

EXPLORATION

Use the Internet to research the competition for a business you would like to start. List the Web site URLs, e-mail addresses, phone and fax numbers, and the addresses of five competitors you located via the Internet.

Competitor Name	Web Site URL	E-mail Address	Phone/Fax Number	Address

VOCABULARY

Fill in the blanks in the following paragraph with the correct vocabulary words.

business definition ■ competitive advantage ■ mission ■ mission statement ■ strategy ■ tactics ■ unique selling proposition

Your _____ is your _____ for beating the competition. Competitive strategy combines the _____ with competitive advantage. The essence of this strategy should be communicated in a _____ . _____ are the specific actions and activities required to carry out your strategy in operating the business. To be successful, you must have a _____ that will attract customers to buy from you. Your _____ as an entrepreneur is to use your competitive advantage to satisfy your customers.

CHAPTER 17 QUIZ
Competitive Strategy: Define Your Business, Mission, and Tactics

1. Define "competitive advantage."

2. Pick three businesses you go to as a customer and describe their competitive advantages.

   a.

   b.

   c.

3. Fill in the blank: A competitive advantage must be _____, meaning that you can keep it going for a long time. Explain why this is true.

4. What is a unique selling proposition?

5. Explain the difference between "tactics" and "strategy." Use a real-life business example in your explanation.

MODULE 2   UNIT 4

6. What does a mission statement express about a business?

7. What are three unique things about you that could become competitive advantages for your business?

   a.

   b.

   c.

CHAPTER 17 COMPETITIVE STRATEGY: Define Your Business, Mission, and Tactics

8. Part of defining your competitive advantage is researching the competition. What are some ways for you to research your competition?

   _____
   _____
   _____
   _____
   _____
   _____

9. List the three things necessary for a business to outperform the competition.

   a. _____
   _____
   _____

   b. _____
   _____
   _____

   c. _____
   _____
   _____

CHAPTER 18

DEVELOPING YOUR MARKETING MIX

CRITICAL THINKING ABOUT... YOUR MARKETING MIX

1. Why is it important for an entrepreneur to be "market driven"? What does this mean?

2. Give an example of a business in which having the lowest price has been a successful strategy. Explain the strategy.

3. Give an example of a business that successfully uses a different strategy from charging the lowest possible price. Explain that strategy.

4. What do you think is the right market segment for your business? How do you intend to learn more about your target market?

CHAPTER 18 DEVELOPING YOUR MARKETING MIX

KEY CONCEPTS

1. What business are you planning to start? Which method will you use to segment your market? Explain.
   _____
   _____
   _____

2. Which pricing strategy do you intend to use for your product (or service)? Explain.
   _____
   _____
   _____

3. What is a drawback of "cost-plus" pricing?
   _____
   _____
   _____

4. What is "penetration" pricing? Can you think of an example of a company that has used penetration pricing to introduce a new product?
   _____
   _____
   _____

5. Bring to class an ad from a newspaper or magazine that illustrates one of the pricing strategies explained in this chapter.
   _____
   _____
   _____

6. Read *A Business for the Young Entrepreneur* on page 249 of your textbook. Describe John's pricing strategy.
   _____
   _____
   _____

MODULE 2   UNIT 4

MARKETING MIX CHART

In the chart below, identify your market segment for your business and develop your marketing mix.

My Market Segment: _____

Marketing Mix	Decision	Explanation
Product		
Price		
Place		
Promotion		

EXPLORATION

1. Visit three different fast food restaurants, then answer the following:

   a. What do you think the competitive advantage of each restaurant is?

   Restaurant 1: _____

   Restaurant 2: _____

   Restaurant 3: _____

   b. Did you see any differences in how the employees handled customers' orders? Describe them.

   Restaurant 1: _____

   Restaurant 2: _____

   Restaurant 3: _____

CHAPTER 18 DEVELOPING YOUR MARKETING MIX

    c. Describe what you think the pricing strategy of each restaurant is.

       Restaurant 1: _____

       Restaurant 2: _____

       Restaurant 3: _____

2. How can the community benefit from your philanthropic activity?

_____

_____

_____

3. How can your business benefit from your philanthropic activity?

_____

_____

_____

VOCABULARY

Choose the best answer from each set of choices. Circle your answers.

1. Value pricing is
   a. pricing the product or service at the lowest possible price.
   b. pricing the product or service to give customers the value they seek and achieving a balance between quality and price.
   c. price-cutting.

2. Your market segment is
   a. all the people who make up your market.
   b. made up of consumers who have a similar response to a certain type of marketing.
   c. people with the money to buy your product or service.

3. Which is *not* part of the marketing mix?
   a. place
   b. price
   c. product
   d. plan

MODULE 2   UNIT 4

CHAPTER 18 QUIZ
Developing Your Marketing Mix

1. What does it mean to be a "market-driven" entrepreneur?

2. What is a marketing mix?

3. What are the four steps of the marketing process?

    a.
    b.
    c.
    d.

4. Define "market segment."

5. What are four ways to analyze a market?

    a.
    b.
    c.
    d.

CHAPTER 18 DEVELOPING YOUR MARKETING MIX

6. The four factors that communicate the entrepreneur's vision to the consumer are:

   a. _____

   b. _____

   c. _____

   d. _____

7. If you buy an item wholesale for $9.00 and keystone it, what is the price you will be charging at the retail level?

   _____

8. Describe two other pricing strategies besides just charging a lower price than the competition.

   a. _____
   _____
   _____
   _____

   b. _____
   _____
   _____
   _____

9. What is the difference between price and value?

   _____
   _____
   _____
   _____
   _____
   _____
   _____
   _____
   _____
   _____

CHAPTER 19

ADVERTISING AND PUBLICITY

CRITICAL THINKING ABOUT... ADVERTISING AND PUBLICITY

1. Label the five parts of this print ad. On which aspect of the product does the ad focus?

   a. _____

   b. _____

   c. _____

   d. _____

   e. _____

   There Is No Substitute For Martin Cowboy Boots.

   Our cowboy boots are designed by Martin and crafted to Martin's exclusive specifications. They are backed by Martin. Continually refined and enhanced by Martin's extensive research and development program.

   Naturally, we believe that there is no substitute for a pair of Martin boots. So we designed Martins to have their own unique look and feel. To be handcrafted to their own high standards of quality and workmanship. To share the Martin tradition of excellence, while being affordable to as many different budgets as possible. Including yours.

   Try a pair on at your Martin dealer.

   MARTIN
   In the Martin tradition.

2. Locate an example of "institutional" advertising in a newspaper or magazine and bring it to class. Explain why you think it is or is not effective.

   _____
   _____
   _____
   _____
   _____

135

CHAPTER 19 ADVERTISING AND PUBLICITY

3. Answer the questions below and use them to write a press release for your business.

   a. What was your life like before you began the study of entrepreneurship?

      _____
      _____
      _____
      _____

   b. Were you having any problems in school or at home?

      _____
      _____
      _____
      _____

   c. What have you learned about business that you didn't know before?

      _____
      _____
      _____
      _____

   d. What's the best thing about running your own business? What obstacles have you had to overcome to get your business going?

      _____
      _____
      _____
      _____

   e. Has running your own business changed how are you doing in school? Has it changed how you get along with your family?

      _____
      _____
      _____
      _____

f. Are you more involved in your community since you started your business?

_____
_____
_____

g. How has your business changed your life? What would you be doing if you were not an entrepreneur?

_____
_____
_____

h. If you could give one piece of advice to students who were thinking about starting a business, what would it be?

_____
_____
_____
_____

i. What are your dreams for the future?

_____
_____
_____
_____
_____
_____

4. Develop a concept for your own business and use it to create a flyer and a print ad. Use computer software or sketch the ad on a piece of paper.

CHAPTER 19   ADVERTISING AND PUBLICITY

5. Create a business card and include a motto or statement.

KEY CONCEPTS

1. What's the most important thing to do before buying or designing an ad? Explain.

2. Describe three ways you plan to promote your business.

   a. _____

   b. _____

   c. _____

3. If you buy an ad that runs in a newspaper four times per week, what is the rule of thumb for how long you should keep the ad running? Why?

4. What is "direct mail"? Will you use it to promote your business? Explain.

138

5. What's your "story"? Write a one-page description of yourself and your development as an entrepreneur. (Use separate paper for this exercise.)

6. After reading *A Business for the Young Entrepreneur* on page 263 of your textbook, write a press release about Marvin's two new initiatives. What angle will you use?

___

MODULE 2   UNIT 4

CHAPTER 19 ADVERTISING AND PUBLICITY

EXPLORATION

1. Find an online newsgroup that might be a good source of customers for your business. Describe it below.

   _____
   _____
   _____
   _____
   _____
   _____
   _____

2. Contact an Internet service provider or hosting service to find out how much it would cost to set up a Web site. Write up your findings.

   _____
   _____
   _____
   _____
   _____
   _____
   _____

VOCABULARY

Use the following vocabulary words and chapter terms to complete the crossword puzzle.

- advertisement
- advertising
- cause-related marketing
- copy
- deck
- direct mail
- graphics
- headline
- institutional advertising
- media
- newsgroup
- pitch letter
- press release
- promotion
- publicity

ACROSS

1. The text of a print ad
3. An announcement sent to the media to generate publicity
4. Free promotion
6. The title of a print ad
7. Putting announcements before the public with the intent of selling a product or service
12. The subtitle of a print ad
13. Non-specific promotion designed to keep a company or industry in the mind of the public
14. Sending messages directly to the postal or e-mail addresses of your potential customers

DOWN

1. Marketing that is inspired by a commitment to a social, environmental, or political cause
2. Print, television, and radio
5. A paid announcement that a product or service is for sale
8. Photographs or drawings in a print ad
9. Together, advertising and publicity are called this
10. A letter sent to individuals in the media for publicity purposes
11. An online forum where people leave messages for each other on selected topics

CHAPTER 19 QUIZ
Advertising and Publicity

1. Name the five parts of a print ad.

    a. _____

    b. _____

    c. _____

    d. _____

    e. _____

2. Choose three types of media where you might place an ad for your business and explain your choices.

    a. _____

    b. _____

    c. _____

3. What is the difference between a logo and a trademark?

    _____
    _____
    _____

4. Why is a neighborhood newspaper often the best place for a young entrepreneur to place an ad?

    _____
    _____
    _____
    _____
    _____
    _____
    _____

CHAPTER 20

BREAK-EVEN ANALYSIS:
Can You Afford Your Marketing Plan?

CRITICAL THINKING ABOUT... BREAK-EVEN ANALYSIS

1. Describe how finding your business's break-even point would help you operate your business.

2. Before you can find your break-even point, what other financial statement(s) and information would you need?

3. Let's say you have a business selling a product for $10 per unit that you buy from a wholesaler for $5. The business has $2,000 per month in fixed costs. Last month you sold 300 units. Write a memo analyzing this business from the perspective of a break-even point and discuss three strategies for improving the situation.

CHAPTER 20 BREAK-EVEN ANALYSIS: Can You Afford Your Marketing Plan?

KEY CONCEPTS

1. Describe why break-even analysis is the fourth step in the marketing process.

   _____
   _____
   _____

2. What is the formula for calculating break-even units?

   _____
   _____
   _____

3. Figure gross profit per unit:

Item	Selling Price per Unit	COGS per Unit	VC per Unit	Gross Profit per Unit
Comb	1.00	.50	.10	_____
Tie	10.00	3.00	.25	_____
Watch	20.00	8.00	2.00	_____

PROBLEMS

Apply the break-even formula to find the "break-even" number of units for each problem.

Problem 1
Monthly fixed operating costs = $100
Gross profit per unit = $0

_____
_____

Problem 2
Monthly fixed operating costs = $1,200
Gross profit per unit = $20

_____
_____

Problem 3
Monthly fixed operating costs = $3,000
Gross profit per unit = $12

_____
_____

CAN YOU AFFORD YOUR BUSINESS PLAN?

1. A business expects to sell 100 units next month. They anticipate $600 of fixed operating costs. How many units would have to be sold to "break even"?

   Monthly marketing cost = $400
   Other monthly fixed operating costs = $200
   Gross profit per unit = $8

   _____
   _____

2. If they sell 100 units, could the business afford to have $600 in fixed operating costs?

   _____
   _____

3. If yes, how much profit will they make? If no, how much will they stand to lose?

   _____
   _____

VOCABULARY

Choose the best definition from each set of answers. Circle your answers.

1. Break-even analysis
   a. the fourth and final step of the marketing process
   b. a tool to determine if you can afford your marketing plan
   c. both of the above

2. Break-even point
   a. the point at which the total at the bottom of the income statement is positive
   b. the point at which a business has sold exactly enough units for profit to cover costs
   c. the point at which a business has made a profit

3. Break-even units
   a. fixed operating costs divided by marketing costs
   b. the number of units a business has to sell to cover variable costs
   c. the number of units a business must sell to cover fixed operating costs

CHAPTER 20 QUIZ

Break-Even Analysis: Can You Afford Your Marketing Plan?

1. What is Michelle's profit per unit if she buys perfume at $3 a bottle and sells it at $8?

2. How many bottles will she have to sell to cover her fixed costs of $30?

3. How many bottles will she have to sell to break even if her fixed costs increase to $60 — i.e., if she spends an additional $20 on a table at the trade fair and $10 on advertising?

4. A shoe store owner pays Brian 5% commission on every pair of shoes he sells. If Brian sells $1,500 worth of shoes in a month, what is the variable cost to the store owner?

5. If Brian sells 100 pairs of shoes, for $1,500 total revenue, what is the variable cost per unit?

6. Find the total monthly fixed costs for a restaurant from the information below:

    Utilities: $300; Salaries: $2,000; Advertising: $400; Interest: $0; Insurance: $800; Rent: $1,000; Depreciation: $300

7. If every meal served costs $4 and sells for $10, what is the profit on each (gross profit per unit)?

8. If the restaurant has no variable costs, how many meals must be sold to break even?

9. Jorge made $100 profit for January. In February, he broke even. In March, he lost $20. How would you say Jorge's business is doing?

10. What should an entrepreneur do if the business is not breaking even?

CHAPTER 21

PRINCIPLES OF SUCCESSFUL SELLING

CRITICAL THINKING ABOUT... SUCCESSFUL SELLING

1. Do you plan to make sales calls for your business? Why or why not?
   _____
   _____
   _____

2. Have you created any marketing materials? If so, have three friends and a mentor (someone older that you respect who can give you advice about your business) look over your materials and give you feedback. Write a memo listing suggestions and what you plan to do to improve your marketing materials.
   _____
   _____
   _____
   _____
   _____
   _____
   _____
   _____
   _____
   _____
   _____

KEY CONCEPTS

1. Explain three reasons why salespeople often become successful entrepreneurs.
   _____
   _____
   _____

CHAPTER 21 PRINCIPLES OF SUCCESSFUL SELLING

2. Choose three ways you plan to sell your product or service. Describe why you have chosen these three and why you think they will work.

   _____
   _____
   _____
   _____
   _____
   _____

3. Write a sales pitch for the product (or service) your business will be selling. Include the features and benefits.

   _____
   _____
   _____
   _____
   _____
   _____
   _____
   _____
   _____
   _____

4. Develop a list of features and customer benefits for the following:

Product	Features	Benefits
Diet Soda		

MODULE 2 UNIT 5

Product	Features	Benefits
Earrings		
Necktie		
Delivery Service		
T-shirt		

5. Using examples from the media, explain the difference between marketing and selling.

CHAPTER 21 PRINCIPLES OF SUCCESSFUL SELLING

EXPLORATION

Visit a store in your neighborhood and let a salesperson try to sell you a product. After this experience, pretend you are the owner of the store and write a memo to that person evaluating his or her selling techniques (without actually sending it). What criticism would you have? What kinds of suggestions would you make?

_____
_____
_____
_____
_____
_____
_____
_____
_____
_____

VOCABULARY

Write two sentences about how you might sell a product or service in your business. Use the following vocabulary terms.

commission ■ sales call

_____
_____
_____
_____
_____
_____

MODULE 2   UNIT 5

CHAPTER 21 QUIZ
Principles of Successful Selling

1. List four principles of selling in the space below. Do not include "knowing your product."

    a. _____

    b. _____

    c. _____

    d. _____

2. You are selling a T-shirt that is 100% cotton with a double-knit crew neck. It has a colorful (and washable) original design on the front. A customized name or phrase can be printed to order on the back. Identify three features and customer benefits.

	Feature	Customer Benefit
a.		
b.		
c.		

3. How can asking for a referral help a salesperson?

    _____
    _____
    _____
    _____

CHAPTER 21   PRINCIPLES OF SUCCESSFUL SELLING

4. What should you try to do if a customer objects to something about your product?

    _____

    _____

5. Which commission would be worth more money? (Circle one.)

    a. 10% on $1,000.00

    b. 5% on $2,000.00

    c. 20% on $900.00

6. What items should be filled out on every sales receipt?

    _____

    _____

    _____

7. Fill in the missing steps of a sales call:

    a. _____

    b. Greeting

    c. Showing the product/service

    d. _____

    e. _____

    f. Asking for a commitment

    g. Follow-up

    h. _____

CHAPTER 22

CUSTOMER SERVICE

CRITICAL THINKING ABOUT... CUSTOMER SERVICE

1. Would it be better to have 25 customers who each spend $1, or 100 customers who each spend 25 cents? Explain.

2. Create a database for your business. Which five questions will you ask every customer?

3. Describe a business that you deal with as a customer. Describe the customer service at this business. What do you like (or dislike) about it? How could the business improve its customer service?

4. List five things you intend to do at your business to offer superior customer service.

CHAPTER 22 CUSTOMER SERVICE

KEY CONCEPTS

1. Explain Joe Girard's "Law of 250" in your own words, with examples from your own life.

2. Why is customer service an extension of marketing?

3. Give three reasons why you think it's important to keep collecting market research even after you have opened your business.

EXPLORATION

Visit three businesses in your community and note how you are treated. Write a memo comparing the customer service at the three. Include such information as: Were you greeted when you came in? Did anyone offer to help you? If you bought something, were you given a survey?

MODULE 2 UNIT 5

VOCABULARY

Explain why customer service is an investment with a very high return. Use complete sentences and use the following vocabulary terms at least once.

customer service ▪ repeat business

CHAPTER 22 CUSTOMER SERVICE

CHAPTER 22 QUIZ
Customer Service

List three benefits of good customer service.

1. _____

2. _____

3. _____

4. What is the "Law of 250?"
   _____
   _____
   _____

5. Write one question that would be good to ask your existing customers.
   _____

6. What do you think is the most important thing an entrepreneur should do to keep customers happy? Why is this the most important?
   _____
   _____
   _____

7. Briefly describe a business situation in which customer service would be important.
   _____
   _____
   _____

Give three ideas for providing good customer service in the situation you described in question 7.

8. _____

9. _____

10. _____

CHAPTER 23

MATH TIPS TO HELP YOU SELL AND NEGOTIATE

CRITICAL THINKING ABOUT... BUSINESS MATH

Try these problems in your head!

1. A wholesaler offers to sell you pens at $1.20 per dozen. You know you can sell them at school for $0.25 each.

   a. How much will each pen cost?

   b. Would you make or lose money buying and selling these pens?

   c. How much would you make or lose on each?

2. You want to hire someone to help with your business for 20 hours a week. The person you want to hire would like to earn $12,000 per year. How much would you need to offer per hour to equal $12,000 per year?

3. How long would it take to turn $5,000 into $10,000 if you had an investment that yielded a 6% return, compounded annually?

4. Figure out the cost of one individual item.

   THE COST OF ONE UNIT

Item	Cost per Dozen Units	Individual Item Cost (Unit Cost)
Soda	$3.00	
Ties	$12.00	
Socks	$6.00	
Watches	$24.00	
Shoes	$120.00	
Candy	$3.60	

CHAPTER 23 MATH TIPS TO HELP YOU SELL AND NEGOTIATE

KEY CONCEPTS

1. Give two examples from your own experience of moments when you either did math in your head or wished that you could.

    a. _____

    _____

    b. _____

    _____

2. Use the concept of keystoning to calculate the retail price and gross profit of each item.

    KEYSTONING

Item	Wholesale Cost	Retail Price	Gross Profit
Soda	$0.25	$0.50	$0.25
Chips	$0.33		
Trail Mix	$0.68		

3. Figure out the cost of one unit for each item.

    THE COST OF ONE UNIT

Item	Cost per Dozen Units	Individual Item Cost (Unit Cost)
Bottles of juice	$6.00	$0.50
Bags of peanuts	$5.50	
Apples	$4.72	
Bags of sunflower seeds	$2.70	

MODULE 2 UNIT 5

CHAPTER 23 QUIZ
Math Tips to Help You Sell and Negotiate

1. How could the ability to do math in your head help you in business?

2. How much does someone earning $5 per hour earn in one year if he or she works 40 hours a week and takes two weeks of vacation?

3. Approximately how long will it take an investment to double given the following ROIs compounded annually?

   a. 12%

   b. 6%

   c. 10%

   d. 8%

   e. 36%

4. What is the price per unit for each item below?

Wholesale Price per Dozen	Price per Unit
$12.00	
$60.00	
$36.00	
$18.00	
$9.00	

159

CHAPTER 23 MATH TIPS TO HELP YOU SELL AND NEGOTIATE

5. Figure the per-unit price from the following bulk prices.

Number in Bulk	Price	Price per Unit
4 doz.	$12.00	
2 doz.	$24.00	
5 doz.	$6.00	
1 doz.	$6.00	
50 items	$5.00	

6. Find the retail price and gross profit if the seller keystones.

Wholesale Price	Retail Price	Gross Profit
$1.50		
$7.50		
$0.25		
$1.25		
$3.00		

7. If you buy a dozen scarves from a wholesaler for $18 and sell them at $3 each, what is your gross profit per scarf?

8. If a wholesaler offers you 10 bottles of perfume for $20, and you negotiate 12 bottles for $24, how much have you saved per unit?

CHAPTER 24

BUSINESS COMMUNICATION

CRITICAL THINKING ABOUT... BUSINESS COMMUNICATION

1. Write a memo for each subject.

   Memo 1: You received A's on all your exams, but your teacher gave you a B+ for the class because you were late four times — but it wasn't your fault. Write a memo to the teacher about your grade.

   To:
   From:
   Date:
   Re:

CHAPTER 24   BUSINESS COMMUNICATION

Memo 2: Your school is hosting a picnic and you would like to supply the soda because you can buy cans for 25 cents each and sell them at the picnic for 50 cents. Write a memo to an adult relative or mentor requesting a loan of $100.

To:
From:
Date:
Re:

Memo 3: You have a part-time job but would like to take a day off to attend a track meet. Write a memo to your boss asking permission to miss one day of work.

MODULE 2   UNIT 5

```
To:
From:
Date:
Re:
```

2. Proofread the memos you have written; then have a friend proofread them too. Did your friend find any errors you had missed?
   _____

3. What information would you put on your business card? Do you have a motto or slogan?
   _____
   _____
   _____

KEY CONCEPTS

1. What advantage does communicating by memo have over using the phone?
   _____
   _____
   _____

CHAPTER 24 BUSINESS COMMUNICATION

2. In the following situation, would you write a memo or a business letter? Explain.

   A customer has written to your business complaining about how she was treated by an employee at your store.

   _____
   _____

3. Would you write a memo or a business letter to the employee involved in the situation in #2? What would you say?

   _____
   _____
   _____

4. Describe the types of communication you plan to use in your business.

   _____
   _____
   _____

5. What is one thing that should be included in both memos and business letters?

   _____

EXPLORATION

The Rumor Game:

Play this game with the whole class to test the efficiency of verbal communication. Have one person make up a sentence, write it down, and then whisper it into the ear of the student to his/her right. Then have that person pass it on until the message has gone through the whole class. Have the last student who hears the sentence repeat it aloud. Is it the same as the original?

VOCABULARY

Write the correct vocabulary word in each blank in the paragraph below.

fax ■ letterhead ■ memo

First, Darnell Jones sent a _____ to Mr. Meenan asking for a loan. He could have sent the document by mail or by _____ . On April 7, Darnell wrote a formal business letter on _____ to Mr. Meenan and enclosed his first payment.

CHAPTER 24 QUIZ
Business Communication

1. In business, why is it important to keep written records such as letters or memos?
   _____
   _____
   _____

2. Below, write a correct heading for a business memo.
   _____
   _____
   _____
   _____

3. What would be the most important advice you could give about writing a memo?
   _____
   _____
   _____
   _____
   _____

4. How have computers made communication easier?
   _____
   _____
   _____

5. How do people communicate through such "servers" as America Online?
   _____
   _____
   _____

6. Profreadd and corect this senence;
   _____

CHAPTER 24 BUSINESS COMMUNICATION

7. Write a proper closing for a business letter.

8. In order to keep good records, what should you do before sending a letter or a memo?

9. If you are writing to a business contact outside your company, would you use a letter or a memo?

10. How can people form an impression of you from your written communication?

CHAPTER 25

SOLE PROPRIETORSHIPS AND PARTNERSHIPS

CRITICAL THINKING ABOUT... SOLE PROPRIETORSHIPS AND PARTNERSHIPS

1. Pretend you are a lawyer asked by a client to explain the differences between a sole proprietorship and a partnership. List the advantages and disadvantages, and then write a business letter to the client.

Sole Proprietorship

	Advantages	Disadvantages
a.		
b.		
c.		
d.		

Partnership

	Advantages	Disadvantages
a.		
b.		
c.		
d.		

Letter to Client

2. Do you think a sole proprietorship, partnership, or limited partnership would be the right legal structure for your own business? Explain.

3. Pick a friend in class and imagine starting a business together. Draw up a partnership agreement that specifies each partner's duties, and how much money and time each will invest in the business. Detail how the profits will be divided.

MODULE 2 UNIT 6

4. Your friend wants to start a business making custom skateboards. Write a memo to that friend explaining the risks involved and ways to protect him/herself.

5. Is a D.B.A. form a certificate, a permit, or a license? Explain.

KEY CONCEPTS

1. In addition to registration, describe two other things you have to do before opening a business.

2. What government identification number must you have before you can sell a product or service? Why?

CHAPTER 25 SOLE PROPRIETORSHIPS AND PARTNERSHIPS

3. What is the purpose of having a form notarized?

_____
_____
_____

EXPLORATION

For the business you plan to start, research the zoning and licensing regulations in your area and describe how they will affect your business.

_____
_____
_____
_____
_____
_____
_____
_____
_____

VOCABULARY

Match the vocabulary words to the descriptions below.

    a. limited partnership
    b. partnership
    c. permit
    d. sole proprietorship

1. _____ If your business involves food, you will probably need to obtain one of these.

2. _____ This is an attractive form of business ownership because it offers the owner complete control.

3. _____ Business owners in this arrangement have little or no say in the daily operation of the business.

4. _____ One disadvantage of this form of ownership is the potential for disagreements between the owners of a business.

CHAPTER 25 QUIZ
Sole Proprietorships and Partnerships

1. What is the difference between a sole proprietorship and a partnership?
   _____
   _____
   _____
   _____
   _____

2. Explain "liability."
   _____
   _____
   _____

3. List three advantages of a sole proprietorship.
   a. _____
   _____
   b. _____
   _____
   c. _____
   _____

4. List three advantages of a partnership.
   a. _____
   _____
   b. _____
   _____
   c. _____
   _____

CHAPTER 25   SOLE PROPRIETORSHIPS AND PARTNERSHIPS

5. What is the greatest danger of a partnership?
   _____
   _____
   _____
   _____

6. Would you choose a sole proprietorship or a partnership for your business? Explain.
   _____
   _____
   _____
   _____
   _____
   _____
   _____
   _____
   _____

CHAPTER 26

MANUFACTURING:
From Idea to Product

CRITICAL THINKING ABOUT... MANUFACTURING

1. Write an explanation of the advantages and disadvantages of choosing to manufacture your product yourself.

   _____
   _____
   _____

2. Conduct research at the library or online to find an important trade publication or Web site for your industry. Find three advertisements from prototype makers, manufacturers, or distributors who could be helpful to your business. Share the ads with the class.

   a. _____
   _____

   b. _____
   _____

   c. _____
   _____

3. Discuss how you would research a new product you intended to manufacture.

   _____
   _____
   _____

4. Describe any zoning laws in your community that could affect your business.

   _____
   _____
   _____
   _____
   _____

CHAPTER 26 MANUFACTURING: From Idea to Product

5. Do you intend to manufacture your product? If so, describe the manufacturing process you will use. If not, describe how your product is to be manufactured.

_____
_____
_____
_____
_____
_____
_____
_____
_____

KEY CONCEPTS

1. Pick a common product you often use and list the materials you think went into its manufacture.

_____
_____
_____
_____
_____

2. Estimate the cost of each of these materials, and then:

    a. Estimate the total cost of goods sold for one unit of the product.

    _____

    b. How much did you pay for it retail?

    _____

    c. What do you think the gross profit would be?

    _____

3. Think of a product that has dropped significantly in price during your lifetime. Write a brief explanation of why you think this occurred.

   _____
   _____
   _____
   _____
   _____
   _____
   _____
   _____
   _____
   _____
   _____
   _____

4. After reading *A Business for the Young Entrepreneur* on page 320 of your textbook, research button-making machines on the Internet. What was the best price that you found? In your opinion, which of the machines you saw would make the highest-quality buttons? Why? Was this the cheapest one?

   _____
   _____
   _____
   _____
   _____
   _____
   _____
   _____
   _____
   _____
   _____
   _____

CHAPTER 26 MANUFACTURING: From Idea to Product

EXPLORATION

Call your chamber of commerce to find out about manufacturing laws in your area. Write a memo describing these zoning laws and how they could affect your business.

VOCABULARY

Using all of the following vocabulary words, explain why you think Ford's invention of the assembly line was an important breakthrough for manufacturing and how it led to modern manufacturing methods.

job shop ■ manufacturing plants ■ moving assembly line ■ setup costs ■ tooling costs

CHAPTER 26 QUIZ
Manufacturing: From Idea to Product

1. What is the first thing you would do if you decided to start a manufacturing business?

2. How did Henry Ford revolutionize manufacturing?

3. What is a prototype?

4. How can you find a company that makes prototypes?

5. Why might you have another company manufacture your product?

CHAPTER 27

THE PRODUCTION/DISTRIBUTION CHAIN

CRITICAL THINKING ABOUT... THE PRODUCTION/DISTRIBUTION CHAIN

1. Given the retail price and wholesale cost of a product, calculate its markup and markup percentage.

CALCULATION OF MARKUP PERCENTAGE

Formulas: Retail Price − Wholesale Cost = Markup

Markup/Wholesale Cost × 100 = Markup %

	A	B	C	D
Item	Retail Price	Wholesale Cost	Markup	Markup Percentage
Watch	$20.00	$12.00	$8.00	66% *
Pencil	$0.75	$0.25		
Pen	$0.80	$0.40		
Hat	$8.00	$2.00		
Sunglasses	$2.00	$0.75		
Tennis Shoes	$50.00	$25.00		
Flannel Shirt	$30.00	$10.00		
Walkman	$15.00	$5.00		

* $20.00 − $12.00 = $8.00

$\dfrac{\$8.00}{\$12.00} \times 100 = 66\%$

2. Looking at the markup and markup percentage above, which is the best way to measure profitability? Which product is the most profitable? Why?

_____
_____
_____

CHAPTER 27 THE PRODUCTION/DISTRIBUTION CHAIN

3. Given the retail price and wholesale cost of a product, figure its gross profit per unit and gross profit margin.

	RETAIL GROSS PROFIT MARGIN			
Formulas: Retail Price − Wholesale Cost = Gross Profit per Unit (Markup)				
Gross Profit Margin % = Gross Profit per Unit/Retail Price × 100				
	A	B	C	D
Item	Retail Price	Wholesale Cost	Markup	Markup Percentage
Watch	$15.00	$12.00	$3.00	20% *
Pencil	$0.50	$0.25		
Pen	$1.00	$0.40		
Hat	$16.00	$2.00		
Sunglasses	$1.00	$0.75		
Tennis Shoes	$60.00	$25.00		
Flannel Shirt	$25.00	$10.00		
Walkman	$10.00	$5.00		

* $15.00 − $12.00 = $3.00

$$\frac{\$3.00}{\$15.00} \times 100 = 20\%$$

4. Looking at the markup and markup percentage above, what would be the best way to measure profitability? Which product is the most profitable? Why?

_____
_____
_____

KEY CONCEPTS

1. Use this form to show the production/distribution chain for your own business, and the markups at each point along the way.

   Manufacturer: Name: _____

   Contact information: _____

   Markup: $ _____ Markup: % _____

Wholsaler: Name: _____

Contact information: _____

Markup: $ _____ Markup: % _____

Retailer (You): Name: _____

Name: _____

Contact information: _____

Markup: $ _____ Markup: % _____

2. What does the expression, "I can get it for you wholesale," mean?

   _____

   _____

   _____

3. Write a memo discussing any concerns you have with the distribution channel you have imagined setting up for your business in question #1.

   _____

   _____

   _____

   _____

   _____

   _____

   _____

   _____

   _____

4. After reading A Business for the Young Entrepreneur, on page 329 of your textbook, describe a business you could start that would involve bringing a product from another area to your neighborhood. Describe the distribution channel for this business.

   _____

   _____

   _____

CHAPTER 27 THE PRODUCTION/DISTRIBUTION CHAIN

_____
_____
_____
_____
_____
_____
_____

VOCABULARY

Choose the best definition from each set of answers. Circle your answers.

1. Markup
    a. price increase to cover expenses and generate profit
    b. the retailer's cost
    c. the wholesale price

2. Production/distribution chain
    a. the four types of business
    b. the producer-to-consumer chain along which a product travels
    c. the method by which consumers communicate to entrepreneurs

3. Profit margin
    a. chance of loss
    b. retail price
    c. markup
    d. profit divided by sales x 100

4. Gross profit margin
    a. the markup from the retailer's cost per unit to the retail price charged to the customer
    b. profit divided by sales
    c. the retailer's cost
    d. the wholesale price

MODULE 2 UNIT 6

CHAPTER 27 QUIZ
The Production/Distribution Chain

1. What is a "markup"?

2. What percentage would the markup be if the seller keystones?

3. Draw a diagram that shows the production/distribution chain. Use a separate piece of paper if necessary.

183

CHAPTER 27   THE PRODUCTION/DISTRIBUTION CHAIN

4. Which step in the chain is not usually keystoned?

5. How do you find gross profit per unit?

6. A video store sells tapes for $30 and buys them wholesale for $15. What is the markup as a percentage?

7. What is the gross profit margin on the tapes?

8. What costs must be deducted from the gross profit?

9. If total sales are $1,000 and $400 is gross profit, what is the gross profit margin?

QUALITY:
The Source of Profit

CRITICAL THINKING ABOUT... QUALITY

1. Write a motto for your present business (or one you would like to start) that will remind you to stay focused on quality.

   _____
   _____
   _____

2. Write a paragraph describing at least two reasons why a customer might be willing to pay more for quality.

   _____
   _____
   _____
   _____
   _____

3. Explain W. Edwards Deming's *thesis* (argument). How was it proven correct?

   _____
   _____
   _____

4. Create your personal ethic and explain what it means to you.

   _____
   _____
   _____
   _____
   _____

5. Write an essay discussing these questions:

   a. Do you care more about quality or price when you buy?

CHAPTER 28 QUALITY: The Source of Profit

b. When you buy something, are you willing to pay more for better quality?

_____
_____
_____
_____
_____
_____
_____
_____
_____
_____

6. Describe the quality-control procedure for your business.

_____
_____
_____
_____
_____
_____
_____
_____
_____
_____
_____
_____
_____
_____
_____

MODULE 2   UNIT 6

KEY CONCEPTS

1. What is the name of the quality prize given out in Japan? Why?

   _____
   _____
   _____

2. What happened in Japan that convinced American entrepreneurs to pay more attention to quality?

   _____
   _____
   _____

3. What does the Japanese word *kaizen* mean? How do you intend to apply kaizen to your business?

   _____
   _____
   _____

4. Give three reasons why entrepreneurs should focus on quality.

   _____
   _____
   _____

5. Explain how Debbi Fields's competitive strategy used Deming's ideas to succeed. Are there products for which you are willing to pay a higher price for higher quality? Explain.

   _____
   _____
   _____
   _____
   _____
   _____
   _____

CHAPTER 28　QUALITY: The Source of Profit

EXPLORATION

Count how many commercials use (or imply) the word "quality" during one hour of television. Count how many use (or imply) "price." Report your findings to the class. Explain what you think your observations reveal about Americans' attitudes about quality.

_____
_____
_____
_____
_____
_____
_____
_____
_____
_____
_____

VOCABULARY

Write a paragraph describing how you intend to apply the principles of quality to your business. Use all the vocabulary words.

continuous improvement ■ *kaizen* ■ quality ■ quality control

_____
_____
_____
_____
_____

CHAPTER 28 QUIZ
Quality: The Source of Profit

1. Do you agree with the concept that a quality product will make a business successful in the long run? Explain your thinking.

   _____
   _____
   _____
   _____
   _____

2. Do you believe in paying more for higher-quality products or in buying cheaper ones? Explain.

   _____
   _____
   _____
   _____
   _____

3. Give an example of a high-quality product, and explain how you would recognize it.

   _____
   _____
   _____

4. Which words best express the meaning of *kaizen*? *(Circle one.)*
   a. Make a product right the first time.
   b. Make it the same way every time.
   c. Try to improve it continually.

5. Who was the person who influenced Japanese manufacturing in the 1950's? *(Circle one.)*
   a. Andrew Carnegie
   b. W. Edwards Deming
   c. John D. Rockefeller

CHAPTER 28 QUALITY: The Source of Profit

6. How has *kaizen* affected Japanese business?
   _____
   _____
   _____

7. How did Debbi Fields of Mrs. Fields Original Cookies conduct market research? *(Circle one.)*
   a. Hired a consulting firm.
   b. Imitated Japanese cookies.
   c. Gave away samples and asked people which ones they liked.

8. Should you ask for suggestions from your employees? Why or why not?
   _____
   _____
   _____

9. Why is word-of-mouth excellent advertising?
   _____
   _____
   _____

10. List at least three ways of working to improve quality.
    a. _____
       _____
    b. _____
       _____
    c. _____
       _____

EFFECTIVE LEADERSHIP:
Managing Yourself and Your Employees

CRITICAL THINKING ABOUT... LEADERSHIP

1. What characteristics do you most admire in a leader? Why? Describe three leaders that have these characteristics.

   _____
   _____
   _____
   _____
   _____
   _____
   _____
   _____
   _____
   _____

2. Write a brief essay detailing how you could find five more hours in your weekly schedule to manage your business.

   _____
   _____
   _____
   _____
   _____
   _____
   _____
   _____
   _____
   _____

3. Create a weekly time-management schedule for yourself.

TIME FRAME (IN DAYS)							
Task	Mon.	Tues.	Wed.	Thurs.	Fri.	Sat.	Sun.

4. Fill out a PERT Chart for your business.

SAMPLE PERT CHART (TIME FRAME IN MONTHS)						
Task	1	2	3	4	5	6
Writing Business Plan						
Financing						
Developing Product						
Finding Location						
Hiring Workers						
Setting Up Office						

5. Do you have any employees for your business yet? If so, describe how much you pay them and how this is working out. If not, describe your ideal employees, what you would pay them, and what their jobs would be.

   _____
   _____
   _____
   _____
   _____
   _____
   _____
   _____
   _____

6. Create an organizational chart for your business.

CHAPTER 29 EFFECTIVE LEADERSHIP: Managing Yourself and Your Employees

KEY CONCEPTS

1. How old does someone have to be before they can work full time?

2. What is one kind of tax employers have to pay for employees?

3. How does incorporating help an entrepreneur put management into place?

4. Write an essay on what you would do to develop teamwork for your management and employees. Use separate paper if you need more space.

5. Describe the trade-offs between being an entrepreneur versus being a manager. Which role would suit your personality and skills better?

194

IN YOUR OPINION

Discuss with a group: Should an employer be able to fire an employee if the employee is very often ill? Before the discussion, prepare by searching the Internet to find out what legal issues exist in firing employees.

LEADERSHIP SKILLS INVENTORY

The success or failure of a business, especially a new business, depends on the leadership skills of the entrepreneur. Leaders are responsible for the effectiveness of organizations, both large and small. They provide a vision and influence the activities of individuals and groups within the organization. Take the following leadership survey to evaluate your leadership characteristics.

ARE YOU A LEADER?

Leadership Skill	Explanation	Range
Rapport	Gets along well with others	1 2 3 4 5 6 7 8 9 10
Human relations	Communicates well and believes in teamwork	1 2 3 4 5 6 7 8 9 10
Passion	Motivated and dedicated to excellence	1 2 3 4 5 6 7 8 9 10
Perseverance	Sticks to task or goal; keeps things on track and moving forward	1 2 3 4 5 6 7 8 9 10
Risk-Taking	Not afraid to take chances	1 2 3 4 5 6 7 8 9 10
Responsibility	Accountable for actions	1 2 3 4 5 6 7 8 9 10
Open-mindedness	Willing to consider new things	1 2 3 4 5 6 7 8 9 10
Able to delegate	Assigns the right people to the right tasks	1 2 3 4 5 6 7 8 9 10
Enthusiasm	Energetic and positive	1 2 3 4 5 6 7 8 9 10
Able to organize	Life and work in order	1 2 3 4 5 6 7 8 9 10
Decisiveness	Comfortable making decisions	1 2 3 4 5 6 7 8 9 10
Wisdom	Intelligent, experienced and competent	1 2 3 4 5 6 7 8 9 10
Persuasiveness	Able to convince and influence others	1 2 3 4 5 6 7 8 9 10
Honesty	Open, truthful	1 2 3 4 5 6 7 8 9 10
Integrity	Fair and gains the trust of others	1 2 3 4 5 6 7 8 9 10
Competitiveness	Eager to win	1 2 3 4 5 6 7 8 9 10

(low ⟵⟶ high)

CHAPTER 29 EFFECTIVE LEADERSHIP: Managing Yourself and Your Employees

Leadership Skill	Explanation	Range
Flexibility	Copes with new situations	1 2 3 4 5 6 7 8 9 10
Understanding	Empathetic; respects needs of others	1 2 3 4 5 6 7 8 9 10
Discipline	Is focused and strong	1 2 3 4 5 6 7 8 9 10
Vision	Able to see the "big picture" and focus on goals	1 2 3 4 5 6 7 8 9 10
Influence	Motivates and inspires people to cooperate and pursue goals	1 2 3 4 5 6 7 8 9 10
Handles pressure	Able to handle frustraton and pressure	1 2 3 4 5 6 7 8 9 10
Empowering	Empowers others to make decisions; shares praise and credit	1 2 3 4 5 6 7 8 9 10
Handles conflict	Has a healthy approach to conflict and disagreement	1 2 3 4 5 6 7 8 9 10
Coaching ability	Teaches, assists, and answers questions	1 2 3 4 5 6 7 8 9 10

Date _____ **Total Score** _____   (low ←————→ high)

INTEREST AND EXPERIENCE INVENTORY

Name: _____

Social Security Number: _____

Address: _____

City, State, and ZIP: _____

Phone, fax, and e-mail: _____

Adjectives that describe you: _____

Hobbies and interests: _____

Future career goals: _____

_____

_____

_____

MODULE 2   UNIT 6

WORK EXPERIENCE

Position 1 title: _____

Name of organization: _____

Address: _____

Telephone number: _____

Salary (if paid): _____

Dates of employment/internship: _____

Name of manager/supervisor: _____

Reason for leaving: _____

Career-related skills: _____

_____

Accomplishments: _____

_____

_____

Position 2 title: _____

Name of organization: _____

Address: _____

Telephone number: _____

Salary (if paid): _____

Dates of employment/internship: _____

Name of manager/supervisor: _____

Reason for leaving: _____

Career-related skills: _____

_____

Accomplishments: _____

_____

_____

CHAPTER 29 EFFECTIVE LEADERSHIP: Managing Yourself and Your Employees

Volunteer experiences: _____
_____
_____

Special work skills: _____
_____
_____

EDUCATION:

Name of school: _____

Address: _____

Dates of attendance: _____

Date of graduation: _____

Degree or area of study: _____

Grade-point average: _____

Student activities: _____

Career-related courses and activities: _____
_____

Accomplishments and awards: _____
_____

VOCABULARY

Define each of the following vocabulary terms and explain how they relate to leadership.
recruitment ■ resume

_____
_____
_____
_____
_____

198

MODULE 2 UNIT 6

CHAPTER 29 QUIZ
Effective Leadership: Managing Yourself and Your Employees

1. What is the most important resource a solo entrepreneur has to manage?

2. How does the Fair Labor Standards Act affect you as an employer?

3. List three ways you could encourage your employees to be good workers.

   a.

   b.

   c.

4. What should you do if you find that you are not happy with an employee's work? What might happen if you fire someone without taking these steps?

CHAPTER 29 EFFECTIVE LEADERSHIP: Managing Yourself and Your Employees

5. List three examples of jobs managers do for a company.

   a. _____

   _____

   _____

   b. _____

   _____

   _____

   c. _____

   _____

   _____

6. Describe two ways to recruit for talented employees.

   a. _____

   _____

   b. _____

   _____

7. What information is included on a resume?

   _____

   _____

   _____

8. What are three ways you can pay yourself?

   _____

   _____

   _____

9. How can a PERT be useful?

   _____

   _____

   _____

CHAPTER 30

TECHNOLOGY:
Science Applied to Business

CRITICAL THINKING ABOUT... TECHNOLOGY

1. Do you have access to a computer? If so, list five ways you could use it for your business. If you don't have a computer, write up a plan for how you intend to get access to one.

2. Create a budget for the technology you think you will need to start your business.

3. If you have access to the Internet, go online and find a newsgroup that would be a good resource for your business.

CHAPTER 30 TECHNOLOGY: Science Applied to Business

4. Do you think it would be a good idea to create a Web site for your business? Why or why not? What would you put on your home page?

5. Describe three things that can threaten computer data. How would you protect your data from being damaged?

KEY CONCEPTS

1. Make a list of all the technology you would like to use to run your business. Even if you can't afford some of it right now, write a memo explaining how you could get access to the technology you will need.

2. Go online and find a shareware version of a type of software that you would like. Write a memo describing the differences between the shareware and the purchased version of the software.

3. What is your favorite technology?

4. Describe the three items your computer needs to communicate on the Internet.

CHAPTER 30 TECHNOLOGY: Science Applied to Business

5. Read *A Business for the Young Entrepreneur* on page 362 of your textbook. Describe an experience you had when you were required to do something or go somewhere that was foreign to you.

   _____
   _____
   _____
   _____
   _____

EXPLORATION

1. Go online and find five software packages you think would be useful for your business.

   _____
   _____
   _____
   _____
   _____

2. Write a paragraph describing what you think will be possible with the Internet in 20 years.

   _____
   _____
   _____
   _____
   _____
   _____
   _____
   _____
   _____
   _____
   _____

3. Do you have any favorite Web sites? If not, explore until you find three you like. Would you order a product over the Internet? What would your concerns be? How would your own business solve a similar customer concern?

_____
_____
_____
_____
_____
_____
_____
_____
_____

VOCABULARY

Use the following vocabulary words and chapter terms to complete the crossword puzzle on the following page.

- data
- e-mail
- flames
- hyperlink
- Information Revolution
- Internet
- ISP
- license
- modem
- Moore's Law
- newsgroup
- shareware
- spam
- technology
- URL
- virus
- Web browser
- Web site

CHAPTER 30 TECHNOLOGY: Science Applied to Business

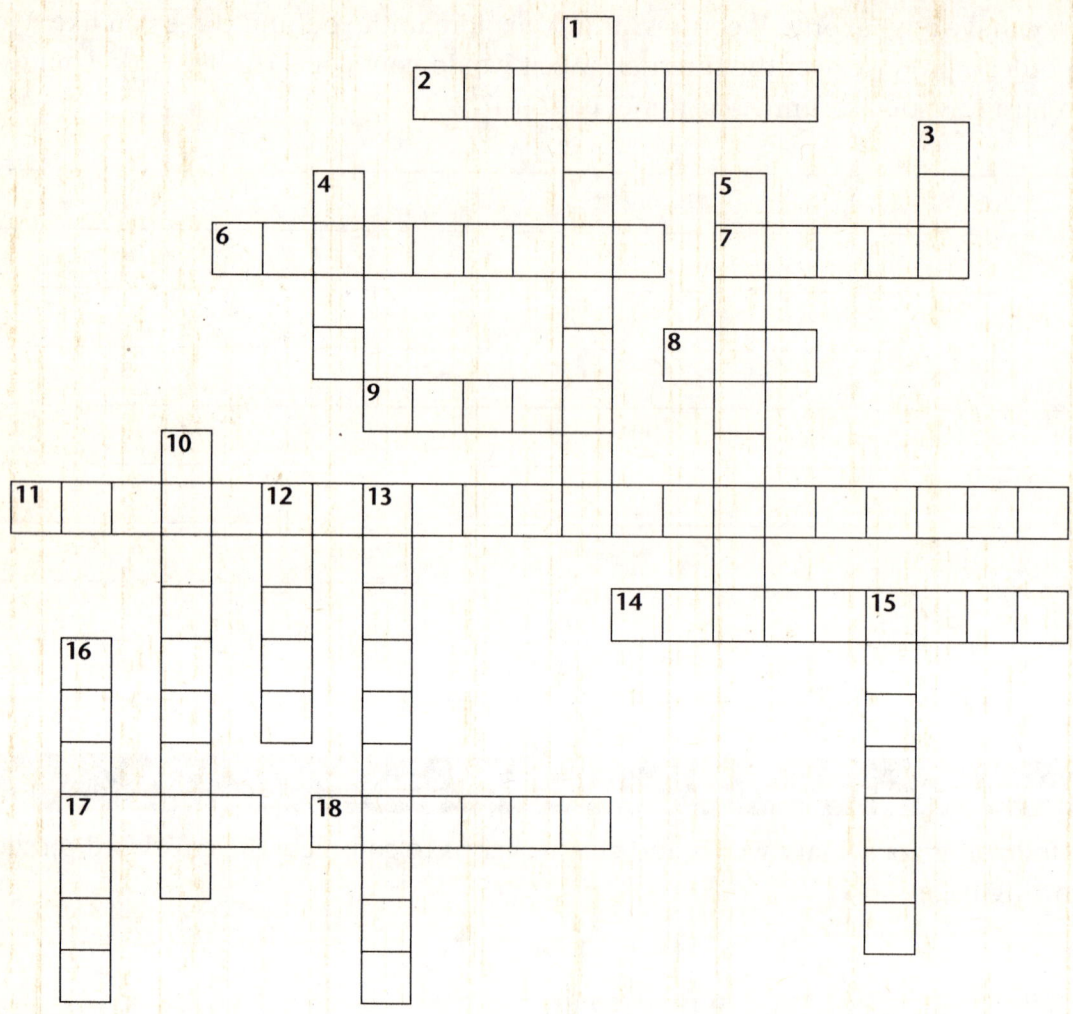

ACROSS

2. A vast network used for sending e-mail, obtaining information, and maintaining databases
6. Free software offered directly to customers
7. Electronic mail
8. Provides a subscription-based connection to the Internet
9. Computer program that can attach itself to software files and hard drive and destroy them
11. Phenomenon of incredible growth in the speed of computing
14. Area on a Web page that leads to another location
17. Unwanted advertising on the Internet
18. Angry e-mails

DOWN

1. Software program that allows a user to access and view Web sites
3. Internet address of a Web page
4. Collections of information
5. Online discussion group that focuses on a specific topic
10. Theory that the speed of microprocessing will double every two years
12. Hardware that allows a computer to access the Internet and send and receive data
13. Scientific knowledge that is applied to business and used by people
15. What you own when you purchase a software program
16. An Internet document on the World Wide Web

MODULE 2   UNIT 6

CHAPTER 30 QUIZ
Technology: Science Applied to Business

1. List three technological advances that have taken place since the 1990s.

    a. _____

    b. _____

    c. _____

2. List three technological breakthroughs you think will take place in the next ten years.

    a. _____
    _____
    _____

    b. _____
    _____
    _____

    c. _____
    _____
    _____

3. Do you think the Internet will replace the traditional classroom? Why or why not?
    _____
    _____
    _____
    _____

4. Briefly describe an Internet company you would like to start.
    _____
    _____
    _____
    _____

CHAPTER 30   TECHNOLOGY: Science Applied to Business

5. Do you think the government should regulate the Internet?
   _____
   _____

6. List five ways that technology can increase the efficiency of running an entrepreneurial business.

   a. _____
   b. _____
   c. _____
   d. _____
   e. _____

7. Name three reasons why a computer would be a good investment.

   a. _____
   b. _____
   c. _____

8. Why is the computer considered a great equalizing force?
   _____
   _____
   _____

9. What will you need in order to be able to "surf the Web"?
   _____
   _____
   _____

10. Name a Web-browsing program.
    _____
    _____

Intermediate Module
Business Plan Review

I hope that I have convinced you — the only thing that separates successful people from the ones who aren't is the willingness to work very, very hard.
— Helen Gurley Brown, *author and magazine publisher*

Now you are ready to write a more detailed plan for your intended business. If you are satisfied with your Basic Business Plan, use those worksheets to help you fill out the Intermediate Business Plan. Consider taking this opportunity, however, to improve your Plan or even change it entirely. Maybe you have decided to start a different business, or have done more research on your costs and can be more accurate now. In addition, the Intermediate Plan includes variable costs, more detailed marketing planning, competitive strategy, and strategies for selling and manufacturing.

Variable Costs

Operating costs such as rent, advertising, salaries, and insurance can be broken into:

- Fixed costs — which do not change with sales. Example: Rent on your store does not increase when you make more sales, or decrease when there are fewer.
- Variable costs — which do change with sales. Example: If you pay a commission on each sale, commissions are a variable cost.

For the Basic Business Plan you may have assumed that your variable costs will be zero, but in fact most businesses do have some variable costs — electricity bills that go up when a store is more active, perhaps. If more customers are visiting your business, they are probably taking more flyers, brochures, and business cards. So your advertising costs do tend to increase with sales, as well.

Even if you don't have obvious variable costs, such as sales commissions, we recommend that you assume variable costs to be a percentage of your revenue and include this in your income statement. A good rule of thumb is to assume variable costs will be one to two percent of the revenue you hope to earn.

Give detailed answers to the following business plan review questions. Use separate paper if you need additional space for your answers.

INTERMEDIATE MODULE: BUSINESS PLAN REVIEW

Your Competitive Strategy (Chapter 17)

1. Use the following charts to define your business, analyze your competitive advantage, and determine your tactics.

Business Definition Question	Response
1. *The Offer:* What products and services will be sold by the business?	1.
2. *Target Market:* Which consumer segment will the business focus on?	2.
3. *Production Capability:* How will that offer be produced and delivered to those customers?	3.

Competitive Advantage Question	Competitive Difference (USP)
1. *The Offer:* What will be better or different about the products and services that will be sold by the business?	1.
2. *Target Market:* What customers should be the focus of the business, to make it as successful as possible?	2.
3. *Production and Delivery Capability:* What will be better or different about the way that offer is produced and delivered to those customers?	3.

INTERMEDIATE MODULE: BUSINESS PLAN REVIEW

Tactical Question	Issues	Solutions
1. *Sales Plan:* Where and how will you sell to your customers?	How to identify prospects and convert them to sales.	
2. *Market Communications:* How will you communicate with your customers and make them aware of your business offer?	How to make customers aware of your offer; how to attract them to the business.	
3. *Operating Plan:* How will you manage your internal operations?	How to make the business go, and determine who will perform the tasks.	
4. *Budget:* How do you plan to manage your revenues and expenses?	What are the sources of revenue? What are the items that have to be purchased?	

211

> **INTERMEDIATE MODULE: BUSINESS PLAN REVIEW**

2. Describe your strategy for outperforming the competition.
   _____
   _____
   _____
   _____

3. What tactics will you use to carry out this strategy?
   _____
   _____
   _____
   _____

4. Write a mission statement for your business in less than three sentences that clearly states your competitive advantage, strategy, and tactics.
   _____
   _____
   _____
   _____
   _____

Your Marketing Mix (Chapter 18)

Step One: Consumer Analysis

1. Describe your market segment.
   _____
   _____
   _____
   _____

2. Describe your target consumer: age: _____

   gender: _____

   income: _____

INTERMEDIATE MODULE: BUSINESS PLAN REVIEW

Step Two: Market Analysis

1. How will you look at location, population, personality, and behavior when you analyze your market segment?

   _____
   _____
   _____
   _____

2. Use your market analysis method to describe your market segment. Roughly how many consumers are in this segment?

   _____
   _____
   _____
   _____

3. Explain how your marketing plan targets your market segment.

   _____
   _____
   _____
   _____

4. What percentage of your market do you feel you need to capture for your business to be profitable?

   _____
   _____
   _____
   _____

5. Who are the potential customers you plan to approach in the first two months of business?

   _____
   _____
   _____
   _____

INTERMEDIATE MODULE: BUSINESS PLAN REVIEW

Step Three: The Marketing Mix

1. Describe The Four P's for your business.

    Product — How will your product meet a consumer need?
    ___
    ___
    ___
    ___

    Price — Are your prices competitive? Do a comparison. What price do you plan to sell your product for, and why? What is your pricing strategy?
    ___
    ___
    ___
    ___

    Place — Describe your business location and its competitive advantages.
    ___
    ___
    ___
    ___

    Promotion — How do you plan to advertise and promote your product?
    ___
    ___
    ___
    ___

2. Fill out the following marketing plan for your business.

INTERMEDIATE MODULE: BUSINESS PLAN REVIEW

	Street Vending	Your Own Home	Door to Door	Flea Markets	School/ Community	Through local stores	Youth Clubs	Internet	Other
Business Cards									
Posters									
Flyers									
Phone Sales									
Sales Calls									
Brochures									
Mailings									
Newspaper/ Radio/TV									
Web site									
Other									

INTERMEDIATE MODULE: BUSINESS PLAN REVIEW

Advertising and Publicity (Chapter 19)

1. What is your business slogan?
   _____
   _____
   _____

2. Where do you intend to advertise?
   _____
   _____
   _____
   _____

3. How do you plan to get publicity for your business?
   _____
   _____
   _____
   _____

4. Are you planning to use cause-related marketing?
   _____
   _____
   _____
   _____

5. Write a sample press release for your business. Use separate paper for this exercise.

Break-Even Analysis (Chapter 20)

Perform a break-even analysis of your business.
_____
_____
_____
_____

INTERMEDIATE MODULE: BUSINESS PLAN REVIEW

Break-Even Units per Month for your business = _____

Selling (Chapter 21)

1. Describe the features and benefits of the product (or service) your business will focus on selling.

   Features   **Benefits**
   _____
   _____
   _____
   _____

2. Choose three ways you will sell your product or service. Explain why you think these methods will work.

   _____
   _____
   _____
   _____
   _____
   _____

3. Write a sales pitch for your product (or service).

   _____
   _____
   _____
   _____
   _____
   _____
   _____
   _____

INTERMEDIATE MODULE: BUSINESS PLAN REVIEW

4. Describe three customers you intend to pitch.

_____
_____
_____

Customer Service (Chapter 22)

Create a customer database for your business. Include name, e-mail, phone, fax, address, last contact, and/or last purchase. What five questions will you ask every customer?

a. _____

b. _____

c. _____

d. _____

e. _____

Name	E-mail	Phone	Fax	Address	Last contact	Last purchase

Business Math (Chapter 23)

Double-check all of the math and financial information in your business plan to be sure it is accurate.

INTERMEDIATE MODULE: BUSINESS PLAN REVIEW

Business Communication (Chapter 24)

1. Which of these business communication tools will you use?

   Phone: _____

   Voice mail: _____

   Fax: _____

   E-mail: _____

   Text messaging: _____

   Other (describe): _____

2. Have you designed a letterhead for your business?

   _____

Legal Structure (Chapter 25)

1. What is the legal structure of your business?

   Sole Proprietorship: _____

   Partnership: _____

   Limited Partnership: _____

   C Corporation: _____

   Subchapter-S: _____

   Limited Liability Company: _____

   Nonprofit Corporation: _____

2. Why did you choose this structure?

   _____

   _____

   _____

   _____

INTERMEDIATE MODULE: BUSINESS PLAN REVIEW

3. Who will be the partners or stockholders for your company?
   _____
   _____
   _____
   _____

4. Have you registered your business?
   _____
   _____

5. Have you applied for a sales-tax identification number?
   _____
   _____

Manufacturing (Chapter 26)

1. What are the zoning laws in your area? Does your business comply?
   _____
   _____
   _____
   _____

2. Do you intend to manufacture your product? If so, describe the manufacturing process you will use. If not, describe how your product is manufactured.
   _____
   _____
   _____
   _____
   _____
   _____
   _____

INTERMEDIATE MODULE: BUSINESS PLAN REVIEW

Production/Distribution Chain (Chapter 27)

1. How do you plan to distribute your product to your target market?

   _____
   _____
   _____
   _____

2. Use this chart to show the production/distribution channel for your own business, and the markups at each point in the chain.

   Manufacturer: Name: _____

   Contact information: _____
   _____

   Markup: $ _____ Markup: % _____

   Wholesaler: Name: _____

   Contact information: _____
   _____

   Markup: $ _____ Markup: % _____

   Retailer (You): Name: _____

   Name: _____

   Contact information: _____
   _____

   Markup: $ _____ Markup: % _____

3. What is the estimated time between your placing an order with your supplier and the product's availability to your customers?

   _____
   _____
   _____
   _____

INTERMEDIATE MODULE: BUSINESS PLAN REVIEW

Quality (Chapter 28)

1. How will you deliver a high-quality product (service) to your customers? Describe your quality control procedure.

2. Write a motto for your business that will remind you to stay focused on quality.

Human Resources (Chapter 29)

1. Fill out the PERT Chart on the following page for your business.

2. Will you be hiring employees? If so, describe what their qualifications should be, what you intend to pay them, and how they will help your business.

INTERMEDIATE MODULE: BUSINESS PLAN REVIEW

SAMPLE PERT CHART (TIME FRAME IN WEEKS)						
Task	1	2	3	4	5	6
Writing Business Plan						
Financing						
Developing Product						
Finding Location						
Hiring Workers						
Setting Up Office						
Other						

3. Provide contact information for your accountant, attorney, banker, and insurance agent.

Accountant: _____

_____

_____

Attorney: _____

_____

_____

Banker: _____

_____

_____

INTERMEDIATE MODULE: BUSINESS PLAN REVIEW

Insurance Agent: _____
_____
_____

4. What are your policies toward employees? How do you plan to make your business a positive and rewarding place to work?

_____
_____
_____
_____
_____
_____
_____
_____
_____

5. Create an organizational chart for your business. Use separate paper if you need additional space.

INTERMEDIATE MODULE: BUSINESS PLAN REVIEW

Technology (Chapter 30)

1. Which technology tools will you use for your business, and why?

	Yes	No	Why?/Why not?
Computer	_____	_____	_____
Home Page (Web site)	_____	_____	_____
Calculator	_____	_____	_____
Electronic Organizer	_____	_____	_____
Accounting Software	_____	_____	_____
Mail-Order Software	_____	_____	_____
Online Service	_____	_____	_____
Instant Investment News	_____	_____	_____
E-mail and Newsgroups	_____	_____	_____
Print, Audio, and Video Brochures	_____	_____	_____
Mailing Lists	_____	_____	_____
Electronic Storefront	_____	_____	_____
Business Plan Software	_____	_____	_____
Computerized Visuals	_____	_____	_____
24-Hour Banking	_____	_____	_____
Tax-Preparation Software	_____	_____	_____
Other _____	_____	_____	_____
Other _____	_____	_____	_____
Other _____	_____	_____	_____
Other _____	_____	_____	_____
Other _____	_____	_____	_____
Other _____	_____	_____	_____

INTERMEDIATE MODULE: BUSINESS PLAN REVIEW

2. Write a memo explaining how you will access this technology.

CHAPTER 31

FINDING SOURCES OF CAPITAL

CRITICAL THINKING ABOUT... SOURCES OF CAPITAL

1. Make a list of friends and family members who might be willing to invest in your business in exchange for equity.

   _____
   _____
   _____
   _____
   _____
   _____
   _____
   _____
   _____
   _____

2. Do you know any potential "angels"? How could you meet some?

   _____
   _____
   _____

3. Searching the Internet, find a MESBIC in your area. Write a memo describing this MESBIC and why you think you (or a real or imaginary friend) would qualify for financing.

   _____
   _____
   _____
   _____
   _____
   _____

CHAPTER 31 FINDING SOURCES OF CAPITAL

4. Describe financing sources that might be willing to invest in your business in exchange for equity.

   Friends and family
   _____
   _____
   _____

   Angels
   _____
   _____
   _____

   SBICs or MESBICs
   _____
   _____
   _____

   Other
   _____
   _____
   _____

5. If you receive $2,000 in equity financing from your uncle to start your business, and agree to pay him 10% of your net profit each year, how much will you owe him in the following years, according to the following figures?

Net Yearly Profit	Payment Due to Equity Investor
Year 1: $6,000	$ _____
Year 2: $12,400	$ _____
Year 3: $15,000	$ _____
Year 4: $20,300	$ _____
Year 5: $18,500	$ _____
Year 6: $35,000	$ _____

   a. In what year will your uncle have made back his investment?
   _____
   _____

MODULE 3   UNIT 7

  b. What will your uncle's net profit be in Year 5?

  c. What will your uncle's ROI be after the full six-year period?

KEY CONCEPTS

1. List the advantages and disadvantages of debt vs. equity funding.

2. After reading *A Business for the Young Entrepreneur* on page 385 of the textbook, describe how Jason financed his business.

DISCUSS WITH A GROUP

1. How much money would you feel comfortable borrowing from friends or family for your new business?

2. Would you rather pay interest or give equity in exchange for business capital? What are the trade-offs of each approach? Would it make sense to use a combination?

CHAPTER 31 FINDING SOURCES OF CAPITAL

VOCABULARY

Match each vocabulary word with the correct definition.

a. angel
b. collateral
c. co-signer
d. credit union
e. line of credit
f. Minority Enterprise Small Business Investment Company (MESBIC)
g. networking
h. Small Business Administration (SBA)
i. Small Business Investment Company (SBIC)
j. Securities and Exchange Commission (SEC)
k. venture capital

_____ 1. A government agency that oversees the exchange of stocks and bonds in the United States

_____ 2. A private investor, typically worth over $1 million, who looks to finance start-up ventures

_____ 3. The act of making contact and exchanging valuable information with other businesspeople

_____ 4. An individual who signs a loan agreement and is responsible for loan payments in case the first signer is unable to make the payments

_____ 5. Assets pledged by a borrower to secure a loan

_____ 6. A nonprofit cooperative organization that offers low-interest loans to members

_____ 7. Government agency that helps small business

_____ 8. A predetermined amount of money that a customer may borrow from a bank on an as-needed basis

_____ 9. Funds invested in a potentially profitable business enterprise despite risks

_____ 10. A private investment firm that provides debt and equity capital to minority small business ventures

_____ 11. A loan organization that provides loans to small businesses

MODULE 3   UNIT 7

CHAPTER 31 QUIZ
Finding Sources of Capital

1. How can you utilize the Small Business Administration?
   _____
   _____
   _____

2. If you received an invoice on March 3rd and had to pay it within 30 days to avoid late charges, when would be the best date to pay the bill, taking into account that it may take two to three days for your payment to arrive by mail? (Circle one.)

   a. March 10th

   b. April 5th

   c. March 31st

3. Why should you pay as close to that date as possible?
   _____
   _____
   _____

4. What would be the two general ways you could raise money for your business?
   _____
   _____
   _____
   _____
   _____

5. If you needed a $1,000 investment from an "angel" and have saved $1,000 on your own, what percentage of equity would you offer the potential investor? Why?
   _____
   _____
   _____

CHAPTER 31 FINDING SOURCES OF CAPITAL

6. What arguments would you use to sell equity in your business instead of taking a loan?
   _____
   _____
   _____

7. List some possible ways you would go about meeting potential investors or "angels."
   _____
   _____
   _____

8. What would you need in order to have a chance of getting a loan from the Small Business Administration?
   _____
   _____
   _____

9. List at least five sources for securing capital for your business.

   a. _____

   b. _____

   c. _____

   d. _____

   e. _____

10. After reading this chapter, do you agree or disagree with the statement: "You don't need money to start a business"? Explain your thinking.
    _____
    _____
    _____

CHAPTER 32

CORPORATIONS:
Limiting Liability

CRITICAL THINKING ABOUT... LEGAL STRUCTURES

Choose the best legal structure for each business below and explain your choice:

1. A DJ who already owns all the equipment she needs to entertain at parties.

2. Someone who wants to start his own record company and has several artists lined up, but no money.

3. A jewelry designer whose work is sought after by a national department-store chain.

4. A social worker who wants to start a program to bring meals to housebound senior citizens.

5. Several doctors who want to go into practice together.

CHAPTER 32 CORPORATIONS: Limiting Liability

KEY CONCEPTS

1. Which business entity should you select? Write a memo to a mentor explaining the advantages and disadvantages of incorporating and how these would apply to your business.

   _____
   _____
   _____
   _____
   _____
   _____
   _____
   _____
   _____
   _____
   _____

2. Is your business a: Sole Proprietorship ____

   Partnership ____

   Limited Partnerhsip ____

   C Corporation ____

   Subchapter-S ____

   Limited Liability Company ____

   Nonprofit Corporation? ____

3. Why did you choose this structure?

   _____
   _____
   _____

4. If you were to form a corporation:
   - Who would the stockholders be?

   _____
   _____

MODULE 3 UNIT 7

- Who would your officers be?
  _____
  _____

- Who would your board of directors be?
  _____
  _____

5. Write a letter to an individual, asking him/her to be a member of your board, and explaining why he/she should accept. Use separate paper for this exercise.

6. Research either online or by phoning your local chamber of commerce exactly what steps you will have to take to register your business. Make a list of the places that you contacted.
   _____
   _____
   _____
   _____
   _____

7. Write a memo explaining the steps and listing what documents and fees you will need in order to create and operate your business.
   _____
   _____
   _____
   _____
   _____
   _____
   _____
   _____
   _____

CHAPTER 32 CORPORATIONS: Limiting Liability

8. Read *A Business for the Young Entrepreneur* on page 397 of your textbook. Describe how a used-clothing shop like the one described could be organized as a nonprofit corporation. What would the owners have to do? What benefits would the people who donate clothing receive? Use separate paper for this exercise.

VOCABULARY

Match each vocabulary word with the correct definition.

a. board of directors
b. corporation
c. dividend
d. donation
e. limited liability company
f. stockholder
g. tax-exempt

_____ 1. A gift to charity

_____ 2. Corporate payment to stockholders

_____ 3. Sheltered from tax

_____ 4. A legal "person" (entity)

_____ 5. People appointed to direct or advise a corporation

_____ 6. A business structure that combines some of the beneficial features of partnerships and corporations

_____ 7. A person who has ownership in a corporation

CHAPTER 32 QUIZ
Corporations: Limiting Liability

1. What is one major advantage of a corporation? Explain.

2. What is a major disadvantage? Why?

3. What would be the best business structure for an entrepreneur who wants to raise money to rehabilitate housing for the homeless?

4. Explain how a corporation is taxed twice.

5. A limited liability company (circle one):
    a. combines the advantages of partnerships and corporations.
    b. allows tax-deductible donations.
    c. is the same as a sole proprietorship.

6. A Subchapter S (circle one):
    a. is a professional corporation.
    b. has few stockholders.
    c. is traded on the New York Stock Exchange.

CHAPTER 32 CORPORATIONS: Limiting Liability

7. A dividend is (circle one):

    a. voted by stockholders.

    b. money given to charity.

    c. a return on investment in a stock.

8. A 501(c)(3) designation refers to (circle one):

    a. limited liability companies.

    b. Subchapter-S corporations.

    c. nonprofit corporations.

9. What type of corporation is General Motors?

_____
_____
_____

10. Kevin wants to sell motorcycles. Do you think he should incorporate? Why?

_____
_____
_____

STOCKS:
Selling Ownership to Raise Capital

CRITICAL THINKING ABOUT... STOCKS

1. Look up the stocks below in *The Wall Street Journal*, and then answer the questions.
   Ford Motor Co.
   J.P. Morgan Chase & Co.
   Colgate-Palmolive
   Reebok
   Disney

   a. Which stock would cost the most?

   b. Which stock paid the highest dividend?

   c. Which stock has the highest yield?

   d. Which stock has the lowest P/E ratio?

   e. For each stock that has paid a dividend, show the math for figuring out the yield.

2. If you plan to incorporate your business, describe what percentage of your company would be owned by ten shares of stock.

3. Will your corporation's stock be publicly or privately held?

239

CHAPTER 33 STOCKS: Selling Ownership to Raise Capital

4. Read *A Business for the Young Entrepreneur* on page 405 of the textbook. If you went into business with Clarence as a partner, how would you feel about him donating ten percent of the company profits to an African nation? Write a memo to Clarence describing how you would handle that aspect of the business.

KEY CONCEPTS

1. Why are investors willing to pay different prices for the same stock?

2. What is the return on investment of a stock called? How is it calculated?

3. Pretend you could buy one share of any stock listed in *The Wall Street Journal* (or the financial section of your local newspaper). Monitor that stock for one week and answer the questions below.

   a. What is the name of your stock?

b. What is the closing price of your stock?

c. What is the stock's symbol?

d. Go online and find the Web site for your stock's company. What is the full name of the company? What does it sell?

e. If you had bought ten shares of your stock on Monday, how much money would you have had to spend?

f. If you sold your stock the following Monday, would you have gained or lost money? How much?

g. Calculate the return on investment (ROI) if you had bought 100 shares and sold them one week later.

4. Let's say you buy 100 shares of Street Scooters, Inc. at $6. Answer the following:

   a. How much did you spend on the investment?

   b. If the stock price rises to $10 and you sell half your shares, what will your profit be?

   c. What is your ROI on the sale?

CHAPTER 33 STOCKS: Selling Ownership to Raise Capital

5. The S&P 500 is a widely diversified group of 500 stocks that are tracked by a long-established company called Standard & Poor's. The S&P 500 is drawn from many different industries. It is so well diversified that it can indicate the condition of the stock market as a whole. For this exercise, find (or have someone help you find) the S&P 500 in *The Wall Street Journal* or the financial section of your local paper. Now choose one stock to follow. Follow both the stock and the S&P 500 for one week and fill in the following:

	Your Stock		The S&P 500	
Day 1 Closing Price	$_____		$_____	
Day 2 Closing Price	$_____	____ % change	$_____	____ % change
Day 3 Closing Price	$_____	____ % change	$_____	____ % change
Day 4 Closing Price	$_____	____ % change	$_____	____ % change
Day 5 Closing Price	$_____	____ % change	$_____	____ % change

a. Which did better (increased more in value) for the week, your stock or the S&P 500?
   _____

b. What were some factors in the news this week that might have affected your stock? What might have affected the S&P 500?
   _____
   _____
   _____
   _____

c. What would your ROI for the week be if you had invested $10,000 in the stock? What would it have been for the S&P 500?
   _____
   _____

Hint: Take the five-day closing price and subtract it from the day-one closing price, then divide it by the day-one closing price and multiply by 100. This will give you the percentage of increase/decrease.

MODULE 3 UNIT 7

DISCUSS WITH A GROUP

Based on your knowledge of current events and trends, from which of the three companies below would you buy stock? Write a memo explaining your decision and share it with the class.

- *Company A* makes a vital part for cellular phones.
- *Company B* has just invented a process for cloning cows.
- *Company C* manufactures automobiles.

_____
_____
_____
_____
_____
_____
_____
_____
_____
_____
_____
_____
_____

Hint: There is no "right" answer. Like any stockholder, your preference will depend on your opinions about the economy and your feelings about risk.

VOCABULARY

Fill in the blanks in the following sentences with the correct vocabulary words.

share ■ stock ■ stockbrokers ■ stock markets

1. Stocks are bought and sold through _____ .

2. Licensed _____ buy and sell stocks for investors.

3. Each _____ sold represents a percentage of ownership.

4. Anyone can buy and sell a public corporation's _____ .

243

CHAPTER 33 STOCKS: Selling Ownership to Raise Capital

CHAPTER 33 QUIZ
Stocks: Selling Ownership to Raise Capital

1. Explain what a stock is.
   _____
   _____
   _____

2. Why do corporations sell stock?
   _____
   _____
   _____

3. Why do people (investors) buy and sell stocks?
   _____
   _____
   _____
   _____
   _____

For the following problems, read the simplified stock table below.

52 wk Hi	52 wk Lo	Stock	Yld	P/E	Close	Net Change
49 1/8	47 1/8	AT&T	1.6	16	49 1/8	–
65 3/8	63 3/4	Avon	2.5	17	65 1/8	+1
69 1/2	47 3/8	BellAtl	2.8	21	55 5/16	+7 15/16

4. Which stock is the most expensive? _____

5. Which stock has the lowest price-earnings ratio? _____

6. Which stock has the highest? _____

7. Which stock has the lowest price? _____

8. Is there a way to make money when stock prices are going down? Explain.

9. How would you use the information in the YLD column to decide on buying a stock?

10. Below or on a separate piece of paper, explain what percentage of $10,000 you would invest in the following ways and explain your thinking: a bank account offering 4% interest; stock in a well-known corporation that gained $10 a share in the last year; a new company that recently made a gain of $30 per share.

CHAPTER 34

BONDS:
Issuing Debt to Raise Capital

CRITICAL THINKING ABOUT... BONDS

Use the bond table below to answer the following questions:

Bond	Coupon	Maturity	Last Price	Last Yield	Vol (000s)
General Motors	8.375	07/15/2033	101.31	8.25	347,275
Bank of America	5.250	02/01/2007	103.182	3.557	49,352
Hewlett-Packard	6.50	07/01/2012	113.180	4.389	50,000
Merck	4.375	02/15/2013	98.639	4.580	47,740

1. Which bond has the highest yield? _____

2. Which bond had the highest volume in trading? _____

3. Which bond closed at the lowest price? _____

4. Which bond is selling below par? _____

KEY CONCEPTS

1. Do you intend to use debt to finance your business? Explain.

CHAPTER 34 BONDS: Issuing Debt to Raise Capital

2. Do you think you will ever issue bonds to finance your business? Why or why not?

_____
_____
_____
_____
_____
_____
_____
_____
_____

VOCABULARY

Complete the sentences below using the vocabulary words.

bond ■ discount ■ face value ■ inflation ■ maturity ■ par ■ premium ■ principal ■ securities

1. The _____ of a bond is the original amount the purchaser paid.

2. A bond may change owners many times as it is traded on the open market, but whoever owns it at _____ may redeem it with the company that issued it.

3. A bond trading at a _____ has lost some value.

4. A bond trading at _____ is worth the same amount of money as it was the day it was issued.

5. A bond trading above par is trading at a _____ .

6. Bonds are different from other loans because a corporation that issues a bond does not have to pay regularly monthly payments on the _____ .

7. The value of bonds is affected by _____ .

8. A _____ is an interest-bearing certificate issued by a corporation or government.

9. Bonds and stocks together are called _____ .

MODULE 3   UNIT 7

CHAPTER 34 QUIZ
Bonds: Issuing Debt to Raise Capital

For the following three sentences, answer either "stocks" or "bonds."

1. _____ are "debt" financing.

2. _____ are "equity" financing.

3. Dividends are paid on _____, but are not guaranteed.

4. Explain the "face value" of a bond.
   _____
   _____
   _____
   _____

5. What happens when a bond reaches maturity?
   _____
   _____
   _____
   _____

For the following questions, use the bond table below.

Bond	Coupon	Maturity	Last Price	Last Yield	Vol (000s)
General Motors	8.375	07/15/2033	101.31	8.25	347,275
Bank of America	5.250	02/01/2007	103.182	3.557	49,352
Hewlett-Packard	6.50	07/01/2012	113.180	4.389	50,000
Merck	4.375	02/15/2013	98.639	4.580	47,740

6. Which of the above bonds has the best yield? _____

7. Which has the earliest maturity? _____

8. Which bond has a volume of 50,000? _____

CHAPTER 34 BONDS: Issuing Debt to Raise Capital

9. Which one would you yourself buy? Explain.
___
___
___
___
___
___

THE BALANCE SHEET:
A Snapshot of Your Financial Strategy

CRITICAL THINKING ABOUT... BALANCE SHEETS

1. Using the balance sheet below, answer these questions:

"SAME SIZE" BALANCE SHEET ANALYSIS			
Restaurant	Dec. 31, 2007	Dec. 31, 2006	% Change
Assets			
Cash:	$8,000	$10,000	(20)%
Inventory:	5,000	4,000	25%
Capital Equipment:	9,000	8,000	13%
Other Assets:	–	–	
Total Assets:	$22,000	$22,000	0%
Liabilities			
Short-Term Liabilities:	$1,000	$4,000	(75)%
Long-Term Liabilities:	4,000	5,000	(20)%
Owner's Equity:	17,000	13,000	31%
Total Liabilities + OE:	$22,000	$22,000	0%

a. What are the debt-to-equity ratios at the beginning and end of the 2006 fiscal year? Has it improved? If so, by how much?

b. The restaurant has less cash at the end of the year than it had at the beginning. Is this a bad thing or not? Explain.

c. Do you think the restaurant will have enough cash to pay its expenses going into 2007?

251

CHAPTER 35 THE BALANCE SHEET: A Snapshot of Your Financial Strategy

d. The restaurant "grew" its OE by 31% during the 2006 fiscal year. At that rate, how much will the business have in owner's equity in two years (on Dec. 31, 2008)?

_____

_____

e. The restaurant added some Capital Equipment during the year. Do you think it took out another loan for that equipment, or did it pay cash? Explain your thinking.

_____

_____

2. Using the balance sheet of Angelina's Jewelry Company at the end of July, calculate all four financial ratios (quick, current, debt, and debt-to-equity) for the business.

BALANCE SHEET (Problem A)

Angelina's Jewelry Co.   July 30, 2006

Assets		Liabilities	
Current Assets		**Short-Term Liabilities**	
Cash:	$1,000	Accounts Payable (AP):	$1,000
Inventory:	1,000	Short-Term Loans:	500
Securities:	1,000	Total Short-Term Liabilities:	$1,500
Total Current Assets:	$3,000	Total Long-Term Liabilities:	1,500
Long-Term Assets:	7,000	**Owner's Equity:**	$7,000
Total Assets:	**$10,000**	**Total Liabilities + OE:**	**$10,000**

Quick Ratio:

_____

Current Ratio:

_____

Debt Ratio:

_____

Debt-to-Equity Ratio:

_____

3. Write a memo analyzing the financial strengths and weaknesses of Angelina's venture. Use the same size analysis below. Would you invest in her business? Why or why not?

BALANCE SHEET (Problem B)

Angelina's Jewelry Co.	Aug. 30, 2006	July 30, 2006	% Change
Assets			
Current Assets			
Cash:	$500	$1,000	(50)%
Inventory:	2,000	1,000	100%
Securities:	1,500	1,000	50%
Total Current Assets:	$4,000	$3,000	33%
Long-Term Assets:	7,000	7,000	0%
Total Assets:	**$11,000**	**$10,000**	**10%**
Liabilities			
Short-Term Liabilities			
Accounts Payable (AP):	$1,000	$1,000	0%
Short-Term Loans:	–	500	(100)%
Total Short-Term Liabilities:	$1,500	$1,500	0%
Total Long-Term Liabilities:	500	1,500	(67)%
Owner's Equity:	**$9,000**	**$7,000**	**29%**
Total Liabilities + OE:	**$11,000**	**$10,000**	**10%**

CHAPTER 35 THE BALANCE SHEET: A Snapshot of Your Financial Strategy

4. Suppose you have started a small business making and selling silk-screened T-shirts. You used $200 in savings to buy a silk-screening machine to make the shirts. You borrowed $100 from your parents to buy 10 shirts wholesale at $2.50. Call these shirts "inventory," which is an asset. The money used to purchase them is owner's equity. Prepare your balance sheet.

BALANCE SHEET			
Assets		**Liabilities**	
Cash:	$ _____	Short-Term Liabilities:	$ _____
Inventory:	_____	Long-Term Liabilities:	_____
Capital Equipment:	_____		
Other Assets:	_____	Owner's Equity:	$ _____
Total Assets:	$ _____	Total Liabilities + OE:	$ _____

5. Create a pie chart illustrating the balance sheet you made for the T-shirt business above.

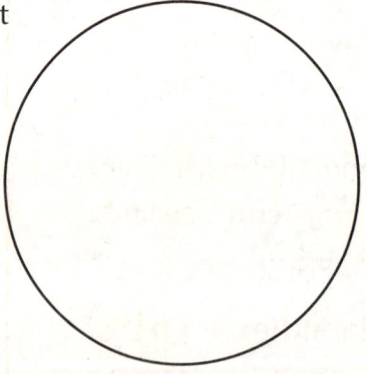

KEY CONCEPTS

1. What is the financial equation for the T-shirt balance sheet?
   _____
   _____

2. What is the net worth of the T-shirt business?
   _____
   _____

3. What is the company's debt ratio?
   _____
   _____

4. What is the company's debt-to-equity ratio?

EXPLORATION

Look up your local Merrill Lynch office in the phone book. Call and request a copy of the free booklet, "The Merrill Lynch Guide to Understanding Financial Reports," which explains balance sheets and income statements in detail. This booklet can also be found online at http://philanthropy.ml.com/ipo/resources/understandingreports.html.

INTERNET ACTIVITY

Use the Internet to find the balance sheets of three companies you know about. Use percentages to analyze their balance sheets, in comparison with the restaurant example in this chapter. Then analyze how they are doing compared to each other. Use separate paper if you need more space.

VOCABULARY

Use the following vocabulary words and chapter terms to complete the crossword puzzle.

- assets
- balance sheet
- current assets
- current liabilities
- current ratio
- debt ratio
- debt-to-equity ratio
- depreciation
- fiscal year
- liabilities
- liquidity
- marketable securities
- owner's equity
- quick ratio
- same size analysis

CHAPTER 35 THE BALANCE SHEET: A Snapshot of Your Financial Strategy

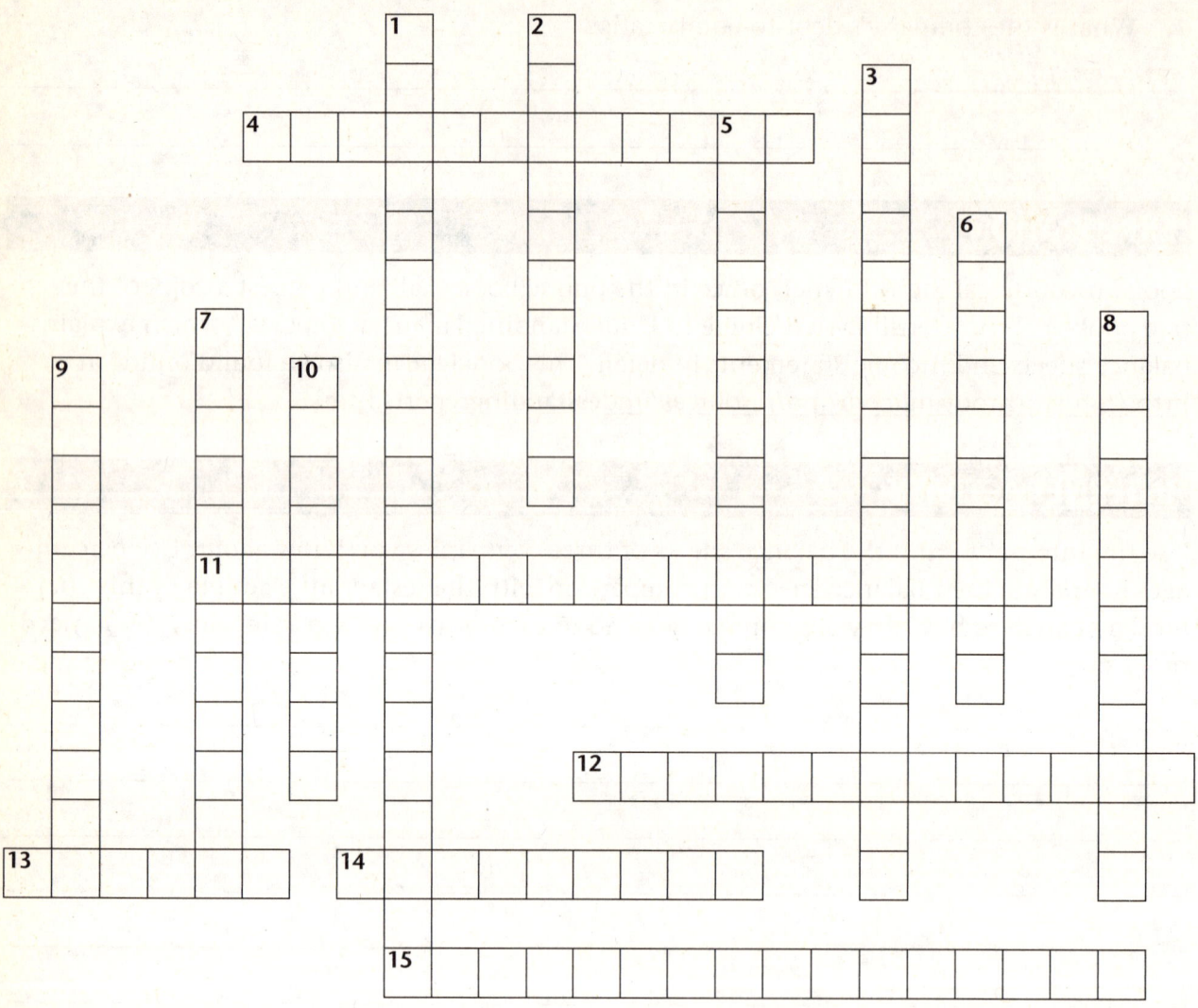

ACROSS

4 Reflects the wear and tear on an asset over time
11 Short-term liabilities
12 Short-term assets
13 Things a company owns that are worth money
14 The ability to convert assets into cash
15 Balance sheet analysis that shows percentage change

DOWN

1 Investments, such as stocks, that can be converted to cash quickly
2 The ratio of cash (and marketable securities) to debt
3 The ratio of debt to owner's equity
5 Represents the value of a business
6 12-month accounting period chosen by a business
7 A financial statement that shows a company's worth at a point in time
8 The ratio of assets to liabilities
9 Debts a company has that must be paid, including bills
10 The ratio of debt to assets

CHAPTER 35 QUIZ
The Balance Sheet: A Snapshot of Your Financial Strategy

1. When is a balance sheet usually prepared? (Circle one.)

    a. every week

    b. when the business is losing money

    c. at the end of the fiscal year

2. What information goes on the left side of a balance sheet?

    _____

    _____

    _____

    _____

3. How did the "balance sheet" get its name?

    _____

    _____

    _____

    _____

4. What do a business's total liabilities and owner's equity equal?

    _____

    _____

    _____

    _____

5. Write "Current" or "Long-term" to complete the sentences below.

    _____ liabilities must be paid within a year.

    _____ assets can be sold for cash within a year.

    _____ assets take more than a year to turn into cash.

    _____ debts are paid over a period of longer than a year.

CHAPTER 35   THE BALANCE SHEET: A Snapshot of Your Financial Strategy

6. Prepare a balance sheet below using the following information:

    You started a jewelry business by saving $200 from your job and borrowing $300 to be paid back in six months. You spent $400 on jewelry and have $200 worth of inventory left. You keystoned the jewelry that you sold.

    BALANCE SHEET

Assets		Liabilities	
Cash:	$ _____	Short-Term Liabilities:	$ _____
Inventory:	_____	Long-Term Liabilities:	_____
Capital Equipment:	_____		
Other Assets:	_____	Owner's Equity:	$ _____
Total Assets:	$ _____	Total Liabilities + OE:	$ _____

7. Figure the debt ratio from your balance sheet.

8. What is the amount of your total assets?

9. What are your total liabilities?

10. What is your debt-to-equity ratio?

CHAPTER 36

VENTURE CAPITAL

CRITICAL THINKING ABOUT... VENTURE CAPITAL

1. Describe the differences between venture capitalists and bankers. Which type of investor do you think would be better for your company and why?

2. If a venture capitalist invested $5 million to help you start your business, how much money would he or she hope to earn over the next five years?

3. Discuss two ways that a venture capitalist who invested in your company could attempt to cash in on the investment.

4. Have you written a business plan yet? How many business plan parts do you know how to write (look over the list on page 428 in your textbook)? Which ones do you still need to learn?

CHAPTER 36 VENTURE CAPITAL

5. Have you found any sources of venture capital for young entrepreneurs that you intend to contact? Describe.

   _____
   _____
   _____
   _____

6. Pretend you are starting the business described in *A Business for the Young Entrepreneur* on page 431 of your textbook.

   a. How would you raise the capital to start the business?

   _____
   _____
   _____

   b. Can you think of ways to expand such a business that would require venture capital? Use your imagination! (Use separate paper if you need more space.)

   _____
   _____
   _____

KEY CONCEPTS

1. What rewards do venture capitalists seek for the risks they take?

   _____
   _____
   _____

2. What will a venture capitalist want to see before investing?

   _____
   _____
   _____

3. What does "majority interest" mean? Would you be willing to give up majority interest in your company for financing? Explain.

_____

_____

_____

4. Calculate the value of a business, given the amount of venture capital invested and the percentage of the company it represents.

CALCULATING THE VALUE OF A BUSINESS

Formula: $\dfrac{A}{B} = C$

A Amount of Venture Capital Invested	B % of Company Sold	C Total Value of Company
$1,000	20%	$5,000
$3,000	10%	_____
$500	33%	_____
$1,000,000	50%	_____

5. Pretend you are a venture capitalist who has invested $250,000 in a robotics company in exchange for a ten percent equity stake. After five years, the company's net worth has increased from $500,000 to $8 million. You decide to sell your equity in the company to another investor for $800,000.

   a. What was your return on investment for the five years?

   _____

   b. What is the ROI a typical venture capitalist hopes to see on an investment after five years?

   _____

   c. Did your investment meet your expectations as a venture capitalist? Describe.

   _____

   _____

   _____

CHAPTER 36   VENTURE CAPITAL

IN YOUR OPINION

Discuss with a group:

1. To finance your business, would you be willing to give up as much equity as Henry Ford did?

   _____
   _____
   _____
   _____

2. Re-read the example of The Body Shop in Chapter 31 (page 376 of your textbook). Anita Roddick says she doesn't hold a grudge against the man she made a multimillionaire. Would you feel the same way?

   _____
   _____
   _____
   _____
   _____
   _____

VOCABULARY

Explain why some investors are willing to provide start-up capital to new businesses in exchange for equity. Use the following vocabulary words in your answer.

majority interest ■ venture capitalist

_____
_____
_____
_____
_____
_____
_____
_____

MODULE 3 UNIT 7

CHAPTER 36 QUIZ
Venture Capital

1. About what rate of return does a venture capitalist expect on an investment?
   _____

2. If a venture capitalist invests $5 million and receives 25% equity, what would the company's value be?
   _____

3. Most venture capitalists invest only in companies that have expected sales of _____ within five years.

   a. $10,000,000

   b. $100,000

   c. over $25,000,000

4. A venture capitalist has 40% equity in a company with an estimated value of $10 million. How much is the venture capitalist's share worth?
   _____

5. Besides taking a share of the company's profits, what is another way a venture capitalist can make money?
   _____
   _____

6. A venture capitalist invested $10,000. When the company went public, she received 600 shares of stock, which she sold at $100 per share. What was her gross profit?
   _____

7. Using the same information, find her ROI.
   _____

8. What is the ROI on an investment of $160,000 that returns $80,000 in profits?
   _____

CHAPTER 36 VENTURE CAPITAL

9. List five things that must be included in a business plan.

   a. _____

   b. _____

   c. _____

   d. _____

   e. _____

10. Do you think Henry Ford made the right decision in giving up 75% of the equity in his business? Explain.

CONTRACTS:
The Building Blocks of Business

CRITICAL THINKING ABOUT... CONTRACTS

1. Brainstorm a list of the types of contracts you think you might enter into during the course of doing business over the next five years.

2. What is the most important contract you will need to run your business?

3. Describe any additional contracts you have, or plan to secure.

CHAPTER 37 CONTRACTS: The Building Blocks of Business

4. Create a sample contract between you and a wholesaler for business supplies.

5. Negotiate and write a letter of agreement between you and a fellow student. You could agree to become business partners, for example, or to supply a product or service for his/her business.

CHAPTER 37 CONTRACTS: The Building Blocks of Business

KEY CONCEPTS

1. Which two things should you do before signing a contract?

   a. _____

   _____

   _____

   b. _____

   _____

   _____

2. Describe alternatives to settling a breach of contract with a lawsuit.

   _____

   _____

   _____

3. What will your signature at the bottom of a contract mean in a court of law?

   _____

   _____

   _____

4. Find a lawyer who might be willing to help you with your business. The SBA sometimes offers free or low-cost legal services.

   _____

   _____

   _____

5. Find the small claims court in your community. Call and ask what the minimum fee is for filing a lawsuit. Write a memo describing the experience.

   _____

   _____

   _____

   _____

VOCABULARY

Match each vocabulary word to its correct definition.

a. arbitration

b. breach of contract

c. contingency

d. contract

e. draft

f. lawsuit

g. letter of agreement

h. signatory

i. small claims court

j. statute of limitations

_____ 1. An informal written agreement

_____ 2. An unexpected event

_____ 3. Court where minor conflicts can be settled

_____ 4. Failure to comply with the contract

_____ 5. Settling a conflict with the help of another person both parties trust rather than in a court of law

_____ 6. Limits number of years in which legal action can be taken

_____ 7. The person who signs a contract

_____ 8. An early version of a document

_____ 9. A legally binding agreement

_____ 10. An attempt to recover a right or claim through legal action

CHAPTER 37 QUIZ
Contracts: The Building Blocks of Business

1. Why should a business or financial agreement always be written down and signed?

2. Is not understanding a contract a legal reason for breaking it? Explain.

3. How can you be sure that you understand a contract and that it will accomplish what you want?

4. Is the phrase "5 dozen shirts" an acceptable term in a contract? Explain.

5. What should a contract spell out regarding payment?

6. How can contracts protect you from events beyond your control?

CHAPTER 37 CONTRACTS: The Building Blocks of Business

7. If a full contract is not necessary, what should you use? (Circle one.)

   a. a verbal agreement.

   b. a letter stating what your part of the agreement is.

   c. a letter stating what both parties will do, with written proof that each party has agreed.

8. Draw lines to match the following terms:

   Breach of contract   a. law that limits time for instituting law suits

   Signatories   b. breaking a contract

   Statute of limitations   c. people who sign a contract

9. "As long as you have a good lawyer, it's okay to sign a contract with someone whom you may not trust." Explain why you agree or disagree with this statement.

   _____
   _____
   _____
   _____
   _____
   _____
   _____

10. When should you use small claims court?

    _____
    _____
    _____
    _____
    _____
    _____
    _____

CHAPTER 38

SOCIALLY RESPONSIBLE BUSINESS AND PHILANTHROPY

CRITICAL THINKING ABOUT... BEING SOCIALLY RESPONSIBLE

1. If your business made a net profit of $10,000 this year, to which of the charities below would you donate $100? Write a short paragraph explaining your choice.
    a. A community garden
    b. A local arts club
    c. A cancer-research lab
    d. An environmental group
    e. Other (create your own)

2. Find a foundation that might support your choice. (Hint: Check out The Foundation Center at http://fdncenter.org/)

CHAPTER 38 SOCIALLY RESPONSIBLE BUSINESS AND PHILANTHROPY

3. Write a business letter to another entrepreneur in your class asking him or her also to donate $10. Explain the purpose of the organization and how it will benefit from the money. Also, explain how donating benefits your classmate. Use separate paper for this exercise.

4. If you could create your own foundation, what would it do? Whom would it help? What name would you give it? Write a short mission statement for your foundation.

    _____
    _____
    _____
    _____
    _____
    _____
    _____
    _____

5. Make a list of social issues you think are important. Find at least five nonprofit organizations that address some of those issues. Conduct research on each. What are their respective mission statements? How do they make a difference?

    _____
    _____
    _____
    _____
    _____
    _____
    _____
    _____
    _____
    _____

6. Do you think the founders of tax-exempt 501(c)(3) organizations would have the same incentives as founders of for-profit companies? Discuss and explain.

7. Identify a social problem and the charity you would found to help solve it.

KEY CONCEPTS

1. How does philanthropy differ from socially responsible business?

CHAPTER 38 SOCIALLY RESPONSIBLE BUSINESS AND PHILANTHROPY

2. Find a company you like that uses cause-related marketing. Describe how it is used and why you think it is effective. If possible, bring in an ad that uses cause-related marketing to show the class.

3. Do you have a mentor? If so, describe your relationship and how it helps you. If not, write up a plan for finding one for your business.

4. Describe three ways you plan to run a socially responsible business.

5. What cause-related marketing do you intend to use for your business? How will this support and reinforce your competitive advantage?

MODULE 3   UNIT 8

EXPLORATION

1. Find a charity in your community and call or visit to learn how you could get involved. Make a commitment to this organization to give time or money every month. Write a memo to your teacher describing your commitment.

2. Write a short essay describing what you think is the most important social or environmental problem in your community. Discuss how you think entrepreneurship could help solve it. Use separate paper if you need more space.

CHAPTER 38 SOCIALLY RESPONSIBLE BUSINESS AND PHILANTHROPY

VOCABULARY

Use the vocabulary words in a paragraph about how you plan to use your business to help others.

cause-related marketing ▪ goodwill ▪ socially responsible business

CHAPTER 38 QUIZ
Socially Responsible Business and Philanthropy

1. What does it mean to run a socially responsible business?

2. Anita Roddick used The Body Shop to raise her customers' awareness of issues she thought were important. Give one example of an issue she addressed, and describe how she used her business to educate customers about it.

3. What is cause-related marketing?

4. Give an example of how you could use cause-related marketing in your business.

5. What is goodwill?

CHAPTER 38 SOCIALLY RESPONSIBLE BUSINESS AND PHILANTHROPY

6. What is a nonprofit organization? Does this type of business have to pay taxes?

7. What is philanthropy? What is the connection between philanthropy and business?

8. Give three examples of services a young entrepreneur could provide to a charity he or she would like to support.

   a.

   b.

   c.

9. Why might an entrepreneur choose to start a nonprofit organization?

CHAPTER 39

SMALL BUSINESS AND GOVERNMENT

CRITICAL THINKING ABOUT... SMALL BUSINESS AND GOVERNMENT

With your teacher's guidance, calculate the following statistics for your class. Use separate paper if you need more space.

1. Class GDP for one day.

2. Class GDP for one week.

3. Number of part-time employees.

4. Why do you think some Americans are worried about globalization? Search the Internet for two news articles about anti-globalization protests. Write a short essay giving your opinion about how you think globalization affects entrepreneurs.

CHAPTER 39 SMALL BUSINESS AND GOVERNMENT

5. Which laws — such as minimum wage and age requirements, health and safety regulations, or anti-discrimination laws — will affect your business?

6. Pick a country and research how people prefer to do business there. Write a memo describing how you would do business with people from that country so as not to offend them.

MODULE 3   UNIT 8

KEY CONCEPTS

1. Why is stable money important to entrepreneurs?

2. How is GDP different from GNP?

3. Explain why entrepreneurs should understand government regulations.

4. Why should an entrepreneur research the culture where he or she plans to conduct business?

CHAPTER 39 SMALL BUSINESS AND GOVERNMENT

5. After reading *A Business for the Young Entrepreneur* on page 456 of the textbook, research the Internet and find three government policies or rules that might have affected Xochitl's importing of essential oils from Mexico.

___

EXPLORATION

Visit the Small Business Administration online. Find and describe a program that you think could help you with your business — if not now, then in the future.

___

VOCABULARY

Choose the best definition from each set of answers. (Circle your answer.)

1. Gross National Product

    a. the annual estimated value of all products and services produced by a country's resources

    b. the annual estimate of successful businesses in a country

    c. the annual estimate of the country's balance of trade

2. Gross Domestic Product

   a. Gross National Product minus imports

   b. Gross National Product minus exports

   c. Gross National Product minus production by U.S. companies abroad

3. Consumer Price Index

   a. the Small Business Administration's measurement of price increases

   b. statistics kept by the government on retail cost of representative goods

   c. statistics kept by the government on taxes

4. currency

   a. money that can be exchanged internationally

   b. money that does not change in value

   c. taxes on the price of imported goods

5. recession

   a. economic downturn

   b. economic upturn

   c. unemployment

6. tariff

   a. the free-trade price of goods

   b. a tax levied on an import to make it less attractive

   c. a restriction on the number of goods that can be imported

7. trade balance

   a. the difference between a country's domestic sales and international sales

   b. the balance between trade and manufacturing

   c. the difference between a country's exports and imports

CHAPTER 39 QUIZ
Small Business and Government

1. Why is a stable money supply important for business?

2. Define GNP. How does it differ from GDP?

3. Why are changes in price important to entrepreneurs?

4. Give an example of a type of government regulation that would impact an entrepreneur.

5. What is a trade balance?

6. Why is it important to consider business opportunities in other countries?

7. What is a tariff?

CHAPTER 40

BUILDING GOOD PERSONAL AND BUSINESS CREDIT

CRITICAL THINKING ABOUT... CREDIT

1. My personal credit history is: bad ____ , good ____ , not yet established ____ (check one). Describe how you plan to establish good credit.

   _____
   _____
   _____
   _____
   _____

2. Write a memo explaining why you would qualify for a $500 loan for your business. Describe the purpose of the loan and the "Four C's" as they would apply to you. Use separate paper if you need more space.

   _____
   _____
   _____
   _____
   _____
   _____
   _____

3. Give an example of a time that you borrowed money (or anything else). Did you handle the situation in a way that established good credit for yourself? Explain. What would you do differently now?

   _____
   _____
   _____
   _____
   _____
   _____

CHAPTER 40 BUILDING GOOD PERSONAL AND BUSINESS CREDIT

4. Jenny wants to buy a used car in excellent condition that her neighbor has for sale. However, she's $1,000 short of the $2,100 purchase price. Her bank is willing to lend her $1,000 at an annual interest rate of 15%, to be paid back over one year.

   Calculate the credit price of the car:

Cost of Buying the Car with Cash	Cash price of the car:	$ _____
Cost of Buying the Car with Credit	Cash payment:	$ _____
	Plus loan:	$ _____
	Cost of credit:	$ _____
	Cost of car with credit:	$ _____

5. Use a mortgage calculator to solve the problems below. When you enter the interest rate of the mortgage loan and the number of years it will take to pay it, the mortgage calculator will tell you how much your monthly mortgage payments would be.

Home Price	Down Payment	Mortgage	Years	Interest Rate	Monthly Mortgage Payment
$120,000	$12,000	$108,000	30	5%	$ _____
$300,000	$30,000	$ _____	30	4%	$ _____
$75,000	$7,500	$ _____	20	3%	$ _____

KEY CONCEPTS

1. Visit a local bank and ask for a personal loan application.

2. Fill out the application and bring it to class. Write a short essay analyzing whether you think the questions on the application are fair and fully capture a person's creditworthiness. Use separate paper if you need more space.

   _____
   _____
   _____
   _____

MODULE 3   UNIT 8

3. Write a memo describing your plan for befriending a banker. Think about everything you've learned in this course — any business plans you've written, your commitments to philanthropy, your personal background, and anything else that would make you an interesting young businessperson that a banker might want to meet.

4. Introduce yourself to an officer at the bank you have chosen to do business with. Write a memo to your teacher describing how the meeting went and your plan for developing a relationship with this contact.

CHAPTER 40 BUILDING GOOD PERSONAL AND BUSINESS CREDIT

_____
_____
_____
_____
_____
_____
_____

VOCABULARY

Match each vocabulary word with the correct definition.

a. charge account

b. collateral

c. credit

d. finance charge

e. installment

f. layaway plan

g. mortgage

_____ 1. Periodic loan payment

_____ 2. Store-credit policy requiring a down payment and monthly payments to secure a purchase

_____ 3. A loan that pays the balance of the price of a house

_____ 4. Anything used to secure a loan

_____ 5. Store credit allowing purchasing without cash

_____ 6. Integrity in financial matters and making payments when due

_____ 7. Interest on the original amount of a credit purchase

CHAPTER 40 QUIZ
Building Good Personal and Business Credit

1. What is a "credit history"?

2. Why does a businessperson need a good credit record?

3. What would be a good way to start a good credit record?

4. When you buy on credit, is the cost to you more, less, or the same as when you pay with cash? Explain.

5. If you wanted to find out about someone's credit record, how could you do it?

CHAPTER 40 BUILDING GOOD PERSONAL AND BUSINESS CREDIT

6. What is the business of such companies as TRW, Equifax, Experian, Dun & Bradstreet, and NCR Corp?

   _____
   _____
   _____

7. Explain or give an example of "collateral" for a loan.

   _____
   _____
   _____
   _____
   _____
   _____

8. Match the definitions below with one of the "Four C's":

Collateral	The dedication shown by investing your own money in a business in order to persuade others to invest in it
Cash flow	
Commitment	Something of value that a bank will take if you do not pay back a loan
Credit history	A rating of how well you pay your debts
	Money that comes into a business

9. What might be the consequences of a bad credit rating?

   _____
   _____
   _____
   _____
   _____
   _____
   _____

CASH FLOW:
The Lifeblood of a Business

CRITICAL THINKING ABOUT... CASH FLOW

1. Explain why it would be dangerous to use only a monthly income statement to operate your business. In the explanation, give an example from your own business or one you would like to start.

   _____
   _____
   _____
   _____
   _____

2. Describe what you think the cash cycle will be for one year for a business you would like to start. Explain how you think the cash flow will be affected during the course of the year. Use separate paper if you need more space.

   _____
   _____
   _____
   _____

3. What are three rules for managing your cash?

   _____
   _____
   _____

4. Describe a situation where a cash flow crunch could develop and force bankruptcy.

   _____
   _____
   _____
   _____
   _____

CHAPTER 41 CASH FLOW: The Lifeblood of a Business

KEY CONCEPTS

1. What are the three risks an entrepreneur takes when buying inventory?
   _____
   _____
   _____

2. What are the two steps to projecting cash flow?
   _____
   _____
   _____

3. Create a six-month projected cash flow statement for your business, or one you would like to create.

NFTE CASH FLOW STATEMENT

Business: _____   **Date:** _____

Beginning Cash Balance: $ _____

   Cash Inflow

      Investment: $ _____

      Sales: _____

   Total Cash Inflow: $ _____

   Cash Outflow

      Inventory: $ _____

      Variable Costs: _____

      Fixed Costs: _____

      Equipment: _____

      Other Outflows: _____

   Total Cash Outflow: $ _____   _____

Net Cash Flow: _____

Ending Cash Balance: $ _____

4. Calculate working capital for Angelina's company. Describe how her level of working capital might affect her business decisions.

BALANCE SHEET (Problem B)			
Angelina's Jewelry Co.	Aug. 30, 2006	July 30, 2006	% Change
Assets			
Current Assets			
Cash:	$500	$1,000	(50)%
Inventory:	2,000	1,000	100%
Securities:	1,500	1,000	50%
Total Current Assets:	$4,000	$3,000	33%
Long-Term Assets:	7,000	7,000	0%
Total Assets:	$11,000	$10,000	10%
Liabilities			
Short-Term Liabilities			
Accounts Payable (AP):	$1,000	$1,000	0%
Short-Term Loans:	–	500	(100)%
Total Short-Term Liabilities:	$1,500	$1,500	0%
Total Long-Term Liabilities:	500	1,500	(67)%
Owner's Equity:	$9,000	$7,000	29%
Total Liabilities + OE:	$11,000	$10,000	10%

CHAPTER 41 CASH FLOW: The Lifeblood of a Business

VOCABULARY

Fill in the blanks with the correct vocabulary word:

a. burn rate

b. cash flow statement

c. pilferage

d. projection

e. shrinkage

1. The _____ records inflows and outflows of cash when they actually occur.

2. A cash flow _____ is an estimate of how cash flow is going to look in the future.

3. _____ is stealing of inventory by employees or customers.

4. A business that has to spend a lot of money to get started will probably have a high _____ .

5. _____ is the unexplained disappearance of inventory due to loss or theft.

MODULE 3   UNIT 9

CHAPTER 41 QUIZ
Cash Flow: The Lifeblood of a Business

1. What three financial statements do entrepreneurs use?

   a. _____

   b. _____

   c. _____

2. Define "cash flow."

   _____

3. Why is it dangerous to run your business using only an income statement?

   _____

4. What are three rules for managing your cash flow?

   a. _____

   b. _____

   c. _____

CHAPTER 41 CASH FLOW: The Lifeblood of a Business

5. Give an example of a cyclical business and describe how its cash flow might vary.

6. What are the two steps for forecasting cash flow?

   a.

   b.

7. What are the three risks of carrying inventory?

   a.

   b.

   c.

8. If a business has $10,000 cash on hand and its burn rate is $2,000 per month, how long can it operate before it runs out of cash?

CHAPTER 42

PROTECTING INTELLECTUAL PROPERTY:
Your Ideas Have Value

CRITICAL THINKING ABOUT... INTELLECTUAL PROPERTY

1. Describe the intellectual property you are developing for your business.

2. How do you plan to protect your intellectual property? Explain why it qualifies for protection.

3. Find an invention or artwork that is currently in the public domain. *(Hint: You may want to do some research on the Internet.)*

4. Write a business letter to the United States Patent and Trademark Office or the United States Copyright Office requesting information on how to file for a patent, trademark, or copyright. Or, if you have access to a computer, visit www.uspto.gov or www.copyright.gov and print out the information. Use separate paper if you need more space.

CHAPTER 42 PROTECTING INTELLECTUAL PROPERTY: Your Ideas Have Value

5. Copyright-infringement lawsuits have been brought against some rap artists who "sample" other people's music. Research the current policy of the U.S. Copyright Office regarding sampling and report your findings to the class. Use separate paper if you need more space.

   _____
   _____
   _____
   _____
   _____
   _____
   _____
   _____
   _____
   _____
   _____

6. Write a confidentiality agreement that you could have employees sign to protect any trade secrets that are important to your business. Use separate paper if you need more space.

   _____
   _____
   _____
   _____
   _____
   _____
   _____
   _____
   _____
   _____
   _____

MODULE 3   UNIT 9

KEY CONCEPTS

1. If you invent a new software program, how should you protect it?
   _____
   _____
   _____

2. What protection should you try to obtain if you invent a new mechanical device?
   _____
   _____
   _____

3. Design a trademark or service mark for your business. How will you protect it?
   _____
   _____

CHAPTER 42   PROTECTING INTELLECTUAL PROPERTY: Your Ideas Have Value

4. What kinds of intellectual property are likely to be most important for you in your business?
   _____
   _____
   _____

5. What kinds of intellectual property owned by others would you be most likely to use?
   _____
   _____
   _____

6. What rights are being violated by downloading an artist's music without paying for it?
   _____
   _____
   _____

VOCABULARY

Use the following vocabulary words and chapter terms to complete the crossword puzzle.

- assign
- copyright
- electronic rights
- infringement
- patent
- public domain
- trade secret
- utility patent
- confidentiality agreement
- design patent
- fair use
- intellectual property
- plant patent
- service mark
- trademark

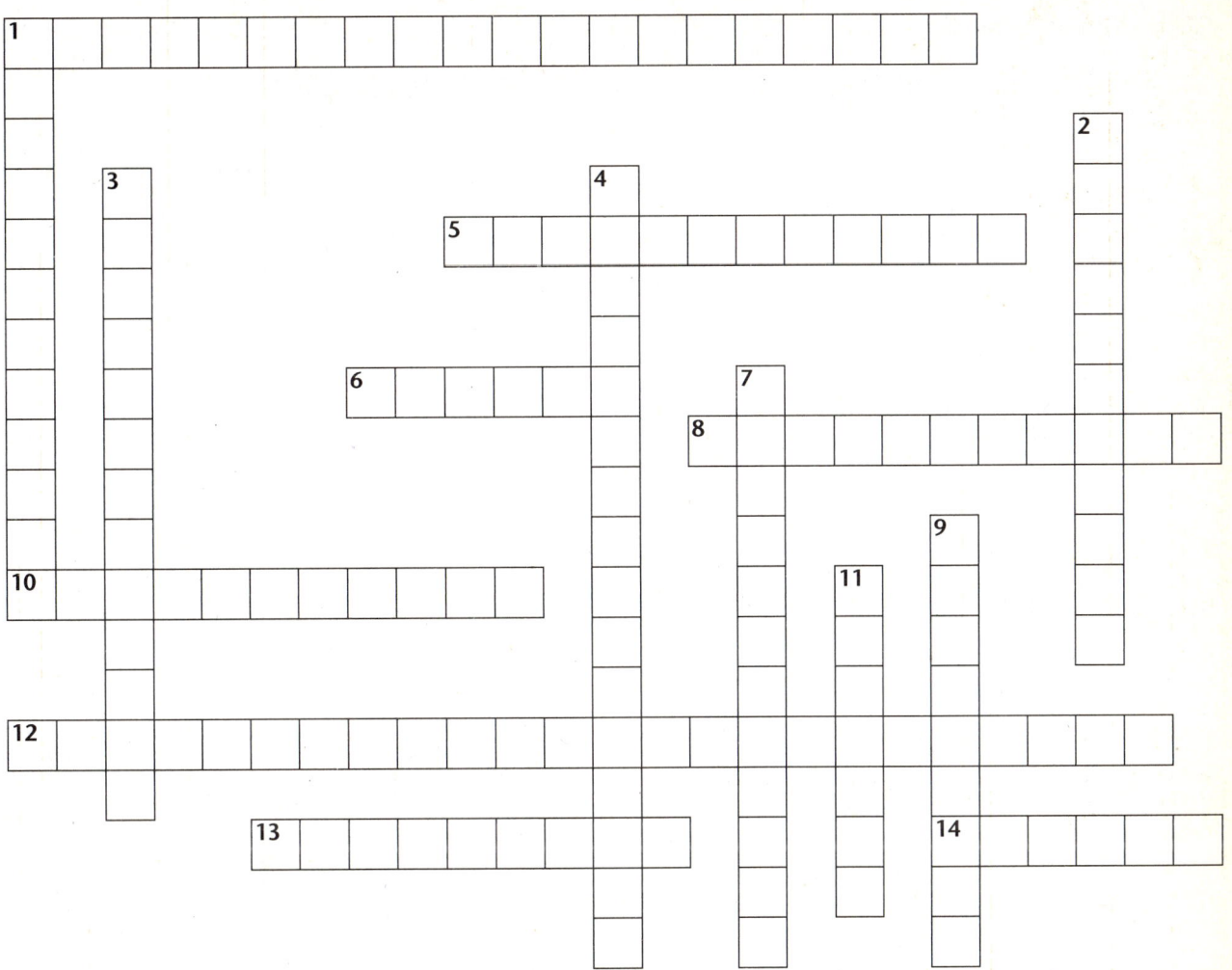

ACROSS

1. Property created using the intellect, such as an invention, book, or piece of music
5. Ideas and their expression that are not protected
6. Protects inventions
8. Protects words, names, symbols, or designs that identify the source of a service
10. The formula for making Coca-Cola® is one of these
12. Document that requires a signer to restrict information and keep secrets
13. Protects the original expression of ideas fixed in a tangible form
14. Transfer the rights to a work to another person

DOWN

1. Violation of intellectual property rights
2. Protects the invention or discovery of any distinct and new variety of plant
3. Protects the invention or discovery of a new, useful process, machine, article of manufacture, or composition of matter
4. Rights to reproduce someone's work online
7. Protects the invention of a new, original, and ornamental design
9. Protects words, names, symbols, or designs that identify the source of a product
11. The use of copyrighted work for such purposes as review, teaching, or research, while respecting intellectual property rights

CHAPTER 42 QUIZ
Protecting Intellectual Property: Your Ideas Have Value

1. What is intellectual property?

2. When can you obtain a patent?

3. What is public domain?

4. Why would a company use a trademark? Give three examples of trademarks.

    a.
    b.
    c.

5. What is a copyright? For how long does this protection last?

6. What are electronic rights and how might you protect yourself against infringement?

CHAPTER 43

ETHICAL BUSINESS BEHAVIOR

CRITICAL THINKING ABOUT... ETHICAL BEHAVIOR

1. Write a paragraph about a time when someone was late, unreliable, or rude to you. How did being treated like that make you feel?

   _____
   _____
   _____
   _____
   _____
   _____
   _____
   _____
   _____

2. Write an essay describing how you would handle the following situations if you were an employer. Use separate paper if you need more space.

   a. An employee repeatedly hands in sloppy paperwork.

   _____
   _____
   _____
   _____
   _____
   _____
   _____
   _____
   _____

CHAPTER 43 ETHICAL BUSINESS BEHAVIOR

    b. After the introduction of a new office computer system, one employee seems to be avoiding his work because he's unsure of how to use the new equipment.

3. It's important in business to know how to apologize if you offend a client, supplier, or business contact. Write a letter apologizing for something you did or said that you regret. Offer to do something to make amends for your behavior. Use separate paper if you need more space.

MODULE 3 UNIT 9

4. Think of a behavior that is legal but that you consider unethical. Write a paragraph explaining why you feel it is wrong.

5. Describe the corporate governance plan for your company. It should include five policies (rules) that will be the backbone of your company's ethics.

CHAPTER 43 ETHICAL BUSINESS BEHAVIOR

6. List your planned board of advisors. Describe each potential member.
   _____
   _____
   _____
   _____
   _____
   _____
   _____
   _____
   _____
   _____

KEY CONCEPTS

1. Choose a corporation that has been involved in an ethical scandal and research that company online. Tell the story of the scandal in a presentation to the class. Describe the lessons you have learned as an entrepreneur from researching this event. Use separate paper if you need more space.
   _____
   _____
   _____
   _____
   _____
   _____
   _____
   _____
   _____
   _____
   _____
   _____

MODULE 3 UNIT 9

2. Visit the Better Business Bureau at www.bbb.org and research a company you plan to use as a supplier for your business. Write a memo describing why you think this supplier is reputable or not reputable. Use separate paper if you need more space.

   _____
   _____
   _____
   _____
   _____
   _____
   _____
   _____
   _____
   _____

3. Review the list of business behaviors in the chapter and write a memo describing your strengths and weaknesses in this area, and how you intend to improve. Use separate paper if you need more space.

   _____
   _____
   _____
   _____
   _____
   _____
   _____
   _____
   _____
   _____

CHAPTER 43 ETHICAL BUSINESS BEHAVIOR

EXPLORATION

Interview an officer of a charity about their operations and write a memo about what you learned. Use separate paper if you need more space.

VOCABULARY

Write a paragraph about business ethics using the following vocabulary words.

Better Business Bureau ■ corporate governance ■ ethics ■ repeat business

CHAPTER 43 QUIZ
Ethical Business Behavior

1. How can you apply "the golden rule" of "Do unto others as you would have others do unto you" to your customers? Give an example.

2. Why is punctuality important in business?

3. How could someone demonstrate the following?

    a. Reliability

    b. Respect

CHAPTER 43 ETHICAL BUSINESS BEHAVIOR

    c. Appropriate business speech

    d. Business clothing

    e. Neatness

4. Why is it good business and good ethics to give a customer a replacement or a refund for a defective item?

5. Can a business be successful if customers don't come back? Explain.

TAXATION AND THE ENTREPRENEUR

CRITICAL THINKING ABOUT... TAXES

1. Why does the government ask self-employed people to pay self-employment tax in addition to income tax?

   _____
   _____
   _____
   _____
   _____
   _____
   _____

2. Do you earn any money from self-employment? _____

   Do you earn enough to pay self-employment tax? _____

   What tax form would you use to report self-employment income? _____

3. How can you help reduce the chance that the IRS will choose to audit your business?

   _____
   _____
   _____
   _____
   _____
   _____

4. How much income tax would you owe given the following tax rates and net incomes?

Tax Rate	Net Income	
25%	$65,000	$ _____
30%	$100,000	$ _____

CHAPTER 44 TAXATION AND THE ENTREPRENEUR

KEY CONCEPTS

1. In a group, choose a public service you think could be provided more efficiently by private business. Develop an argument for replacing this service with a private business and present it to the class. Have the class vote on your proposal.

   _____
   _____
   _____
   _____
   _____
   _____
   _____
   _____
   _____
   _____

2. Fill out tax forms provided by your teacher.

3. Which tax forms will you have to fill out for your business?

   ____ 1040 U.S. Individual Tax Return

   ____ Schedule C, Profit or Loss from Business

   ____ Schedule SE, Self-Employment Tax

   ____ Quarterly Sales and Use Tax Return

VOCABULARY

Choose the best definition from each set of answers. Circle your answers.

1. audit
   a. end-of-the-year bookkeeping
   b. formal investigation of a taxpayer's accounts by the IRS
   c. business tax on auditory equipment

2. Internal Revenue Service
    a. state taxation bureau
    b. federal taxation bureau
    c. local government board in charge of taxation

3. sales tax
    a. tax on profit
    b. tax on manufacturing
    c. tax on consumption

4. self-employment tax
    a. a tax on earnings from self-employment
    b. a substitute for Social Security tax for self-employed people
    c. both a and b are correct

5. Social Security
    a. a federal program that provides benefits to elderly and disabled people
    b. a federal program that provides business insurance
    c. a federal program that provides employment security

6. tax
    a. the percentage of sales taken by the government
    b. the percentage of net profit taken by the government
    c. the percentage of gross profit taken by the government

7. tax evasion
    a. late filing of tax return
    b. inability to pay tax bill
    c. deliberate failure to file taxes

CHAPTER 44 QUIZ
Taxation and the Entrepreneur

1. If the state sales tax is 8%, how much would be added to the cost of a $100 item?
   _____

2. Property taxes are paid to (circle one):
   a. the federal government.
   b. state and city (or town) government.
   c. city (or town) government.

3. Income taxes can be paid to (circle one):
   a. state government.
   b. the federal government.
   c. federal government and state and city governments.

4. If you were self-employed, which two types of taxes would you pay to the federal government? (Circle one.)
   a. income tax and self-employment tax.
   b. property tax and sales tax.
   c. capital gains tax.

5. You must file an income tax return if you are single, under 65, and earn more than:
   a. $400.
   b. $10,000.
   c. $5,550.

6. The tax code stays the same every year.   True _____   False _____

7. The Schedule C form is for taxes on income from a business.   True _____   False _____

8. When the Internal Revenue Service checks your tax reporting, it is called:
   a. a refund.
   b. an audit.
   c. a penalty.

9. What kind of questions would help you decide whether the government is doing a good job setting tax rates and spending money? (Use separate paper for this question.)

CHAPTER 45

INSURANCE:
Protection from the Unexpected

CRITICAL THINKING ABOUT... INSURANCE

1. Imagine that a small hardware store with several employees is destroyed by fire. What types of insurance should the store owner have carried, and why?

2. Explain how insurance companies make money, even though they sometimes have to make large payouts.

3. What types of insurance will your business need, and why? What is the highest deductible you feel you can afford?

CHAPTER 45 INSURANCE: Protection from the Unexpected

4. Pick one type of insurance you would like to have for your business and find a company online that sells it. Describe the premium, deductible, and payout.

KEY CONCEPTS

1. Some businesses do sell products and services that can injure customers. List three examples and explain how these companies might use insurance to stay in business.

2. Choose one of the companies you listed in number 1 and research news stories about it on the Internet. Find out if the company ever had to pay customers who were injured using its products or services. Report your findings to the class.

318

3. Mandy is buying an old van from her brother to start her flower-basket delivery service. She planned to buy auto insurance, in case she ever got into an accident. She finds out that type of insurance will cost her $3,000 per year, which is more than she can afford. What do you think Mandy should do?

EXPLORATION

Interview an entrepreneur about his or her insurance policies. Ask how that kind of insurance was decided on and whether there are large or small deductibles. Present a report on your entrepreneur's insurance plan to the class.

CHAPTER 45 INSURANCE: Protection from the Unexpected

VOCABULARY

Write in the vocabulary word that best completes each sentence.

deductible ■ fraud ■ insurance ■ insurance agent ■ insurance policy ■ liability insurance ■ premium

1. _____ , or the failure to inform a customer of potential damage from a product or service, is one of the most unethical things a business owner can do.

2. To keep your insurance policy active, you must always pay your _____ .

3. A(n) _____ can help you determine your insurance needs.

4. If you have an accident that causes $2,000 worth of damage to your car, but your _____ is $500, your auto-insurance policy will pay you $1,500.

5. If you sell anything that could injure a customer, you need _____ .

6. Business owners protect their businesses from disaster with _____ .

7. The _____ is a contract between you and the insurance company that obligates you to pay a premium in return for coverage.

CHAPTER 45 QUIZ

Insurance: Protection from the Unexpected

1. What is the purpose of insurance?

2. The payment you make in order to keep your insurance policy is called a _____.

3. The amount of money that you must pay on your own, before the insurance company will pay the balance, is called a _____.

4. How could a young person choose a business that would keep insurance costs down?

5. Why do companies have to inform you about the risks of a product or service?

CHAPTER 45 INSURANCE: Protection from the Unexpected

6. If you use a car for your business, would liability insurance be enough to carry? Explain.

7. If an entrepreneur opened a retail shop, what type of insurance would be needed?

8. If an entrepreneur hired an employee, what additional insurance would be needed?

9. How do insurance companies make their money?

10. If you carried a high deductible on your insurance policy, how would it affect the cost of your premium?

FRANCHISING AND LICENSING:
The Power of the Brand

CRITICAL THINKING ABOUT... FRANCHISING

1. Would you be interested in running a franchise? Why or why not? Write a memo analyzing the advantages and disadvantages. Use separate paper if you need more space.

2. Find an item that you wear or use that involves licensing. Write a memo analyzing the licensing strategy's weaknesses and strengths. Use separate paper if you need more space.

CHAPTER 46 FRANCHISING AND LICENSING: The Power of the Brand

3. Do you plan eventually to franchise your business, or license any of your products? Explain.

_____
_____
_____
_____
_____
_____
_____
_____
_____

4. For each franchise in the table, use this formula to calculate how much you would owe the franchisor in royalties if you made one million dollars in sales:

Royalties = Royalty Fee × Sales

Franchise	Franchise Fee	Start-Up Costs	Royalty Fee	Royalties Owed
McDonald's	$45,000	$489,000 – $1.5 million	12.5%	$ _____
Arby's LLC	$25,000 – $37,500	$333,000 – $2 million	4%	$ _____
GNC Franchising Inc.	$30,000	$132,000 – $182,000	6%	$ _____
Tastee-Freez LLC	$5,000	$39,000	4%	$ _____

KEY CONCEPTS

1. Why do you think a franchising agreement would include a "non-compete" clause?

_____
_____
_____
_____

MODULE 3 UNIT 10

2. Write a brief description of the differences between branding, franchising, and licensing.

   a. _____

   b. _____

   c. _____

3. What did Ray Kroc do with his franchisees that was unique?

   _____

325

CHAPTER 46 FRANCHISING AND LICENSING: The Power of the Brand

VOCABULARY

Match each vocabulary word with the correct definition.

a. franchise
b. franchisee
c. franchisor
d. licensing
e. licensee
f. licensor
g. royalty

_____ 1. An already developed business concept and system

_____ 2. Person who develops a franchise or company that sells franchises

_____ 3. A person or business that buys rights to a name or trademark

_____ 4. Person who buys a franchise unit

_____ 5. Authorizing others to use one's name or trademark

_____ 6. A percentage share of the proceeds of the sale of a product

_____ 7. Person or business receiving payment for allowing use of name or trademark

MODULE 3 UNIT 10

CHAPTER 46 QUIZ
Franchising and Licensing: The Power of the Brand

1. From your personal or business life, give an example of a mutually beneficial relationship.

2. Why does a franchise need to benefit both the franchisor and franchisee?

3. Which franchise did Ray Kroc start?

4. Name two companies that offer special financing to help minorities open franchises.

5. Explain the difference between licensing and franchising.

CHAPTER 46   FRANCHISING AND LICENSING: The Power of the Brand

6. Give an example of a "non-compete" clause.

7. What are franchise "royalties"? To whom are they paid?

8. Name two benefits enjoyed by a franchisee.

9. Name a problem or drawback that can affect a franchisor.

10. Name a problem or drawback that can affect a franchisee.

CHAPTER 47

INTERNATIONAL OPPORTUNITIES

CRITICAL THINKING ABOUT... INTERNATIONAL OPPORTUNITIES

1. If the FX rate between the U.S. dollar and the Japanese yen is 1:119, how many yen will it take to equal $20?

   _____
   _____
   _____

2. If the FX rate between the Japanese yen and the euro is 189.35:1, how many yen will equal €10?

   _____
   _____
   _____

3. You own a small record label. You sell CDs through your Web site for $15, including shipping and handling. You get an e-mail from someone who owns a store in France who would like to sell your CDs. He wants to buy them at $10 each and sell them at €30. He says his profit from each sale would be €12 and he will split it with you.

   Assuming the exchange rate between the dollar and the euro is $1 = €2:

   a. How much profit would you get from the sale of each CD in the French store?

      _____
      _____

   b. How much is that profit in dollars?

      _____
      _____

   c. Is this a good business opportunity for you? Why or why not?

      _____
      _____
      _____

CHAPTER 47 INTERNATIONAL OPPORTUNITIES

d. If the FX rate between the dollar and the euro fell to $1 = €1, would this be a good business opportunity for you? Why or why not?

_____
_____
_____

4. Do you think there might be customers for your business in other countries? How would you reach them?

_____
_____
_____
_____
_____
_____
_____
_____
_____

5. Describe any international competitors you have found who may be able to access your customers. How do you intend to compete?

_____
_____
_____
_____
_____
_____
_____
_____
_____
_____

MODULE 3 UNIT 10

KEY CONCEPTS

1. Examine the labels on your shoes, clothing, or household items and note which were made in foreign countries. How many dollars per hour do you think the people earned who made these items? Why do you think the companies that manufactured the products had them made in those countries?

2. Some people argue that free trade is not a good idea because American companies can now move their factories to Mexico, where wages are much lower. Research this issue on the Internet and write a short essay exploring the pros and cons of free trade. Use separate paper if you need more space.

CHAPTER 47 INTERNATIONAL OPPORTUNITIES

3. Answer the following question in a brief essay: "Some American companies have been pressured by political groups to raise the wages they pay to their workers in other countries. Do you think this pressure is fair or not?" Use separate paper if you need more space.

   _____
   _____
   _____
   _____
   _____
   _____
   _____
   _____
   _____

4. Does your school offer an exchange program that would enable you to go to school in another country for a semester? Research exchange programs or come up with another plan that would enable you to visit a foreign country.

   _____
   _____
   _____
   _____
   _____
   _____
   _____
   _____
   _____
   _____

5. Conduct the interview outlined below with a parent, guardian, grandparent, or other adult family member or friend to find out what kind of currency was used in the country or countries they came from. Add your own questions if you wish.

   Family member interviewed: _____ *(Relationship)*

a. Where did you or your parents/grandparents/great grandparents live before moving to this country?

_____
_____
_____

b. What were some of the currencies our ancestors used?

_____
_____
_____

c. Do you have any examples of a currency that I could show my class?

_____
_____
_____

d. Other (make up one or more questions).

_____
_____
_____

VOCABULARY

Explain why entrepreneurs look for opportunities, not just in their own backyards, but around the world. What issues does an entrepreneur face when doing business internationally? Use the vocabulary words in your answer. Use separate paper if you need more space.

export ■ foreign exchange rate ■ import ■ quota ■ tariff ■ trade barrier

_____
_____
_____
_____
_____

CHAPTER 47 QUIZ
International Opportunities

1. What is the difference between importing and exporting?

2. List two types of trade barriers.

3. What are two ways that trade barriers have been removed between some countries in recent years?

4. Convert the following currency amounts, using the given exchange rate, into U.S. dollars:

Foreign currency amount	FX	Value in U.S. Dollars
25 euro	1.23	$ _____
150 Argentine pesos	0.33	$ _____
200 Australian dollars	0.72	$ _____
80 British pounds	1.82	$ _____
250 Singapore dollars	0.58	$ _____

5. List one cultural difference an entrepreneur might need to be aware of when doing business in a foreign country and what the entrepreneur should do to be prepared.

6. List two brands that are imported to the U.S. from another country.

7. List two brands that are exported from the U.S. to other countries.

CHAPTER 48

INVESTMENT GOALS AND RISK TOLERANCE

CRITICAL THINKING ABOUT... INVESTMENT GOALS AND RISK TOLERANCE

1. If Gina earns $50 per week babysitting, how much would she have left to spend each week after saving ten percent? How much would she save in a month?
   _____
   _____

2. Think of an item you would like to buy. Answer the following questions to develop a plan for saving up to buy it.

   a. How much does this item cost?
      _____
      _____

   b. How much money do I make each week?
      _____
      _____

   c. If I put ten percent of that money aside, how much would I be saving weekly?
      _____
      _____

   d. How long would it take to save enough money to buy the item?
      _____
      _____

3. Describe your risk tolerance. What are some of the factors that affect your risk tolerance?
   _____
   _____

4. What are your financial goals... one year from now?
   _____
   _____

CHAPTER 48 INVESTMENT GOALS AND RISK TOLERANCE

five years from now?
_____
_____

ten years from now?
_____
_____

twenty years from now?
_____
_____

5. I plan to save ___ % of my net income to achieve personal financial goals.

   My primary financial goal is _____ .

   My investment risk tolerance is (low, medium, high) _____ .

KEY CONCEPTS

1. Buying a home:

   a. How much will you need to save in order to buy a home? You will need a down payment to secure a mortgage, which is a loan from a bank to purchase a home. The down payment is often ten percent of the price. So, with a down payment of $15,000, you could probably buy a $150,000 home.
   _____
   _____

   b. I have ___ years to save for my first home.

   I can invest for my home in (circle the answer that applies):

   1. stocks (I have more than ten years to invest for this goal).
   2. bonds (I have fewer than ten years to invest for this goal).
   3. I plan to save a down payment of $ _____ so that I can buy my first home at age ___ for $ _____ .

2. Saving for college:

   a. What do you plan as a career? Fill in the blanks.

MODULE 3 UNIT 10

    I plan to work toward a career as a _____ with a starting annual salary of $ _____ .

b. Do you know how much education you will need for your chosen career? If not, do research online or ask a teacher, parent, or mentor. Describe the results of your investigation.

_____

_____

_____

c. How much money will it take for you to achieve the education you desire? (Again, do research online or get help from a teacher, parent, or mentor.)

_____

_____

_____

d. Do you know of any scholarship opportunities you could apply for? If not, how could you find out about some?

_____

_____

_____

VOCABULARY

Fill in the blanks in the following sentences with the correct vocabulary words.

diversification ■ index fund ■ interest ■ investment ■ mutual fund

1. Compound _____ is the money you earn on the interest that you earned in a previous period.

2. Spreading your money over different types of investments to reduce risk is _____ .

3. A(n) _____ is not managed because it is designed to buy and hold stocks in the same proportions as an index.

4. A(n) _____ is something you buy with your savings that you hope will earn money.

5. When you buy into a(n) _____ , you are buying shares in that fund, which probably owns hundreds of stocks or bonds.

CHAPTER 48 QUIZ
Investment Goals and Risk Tolerance

1. How much money will you have in the bank at the end of one year on a deposit of $1,000 at a 6% interest rate?
   _____
   _____
   _____

2. Compound interest means (circle one):
   a. You earn a double return.
   b. You are paid interest four times a year.
   c. You are paid interest on your investment plus interest on the interest.

3. How long will it take for $120 to double if the return on investment is 12%?
   _____

4. Give three reasons why it is better to have your money now than to receive that same amount in the future.
   _____
   _____
   _____

For problems 5-7, use the N-Chart for Future Value of Money.

5. $100 for 5 periods at 5% _____

6. $1 for 10 periods at 12% _____

7. $1,000 for 11 periods at 6% _____

For problems 8-10, use the N-Chart for Present Value of Money.

8. $1 at 4% for 5 periods _____

9. $100 at 7% for 10 periods _____

10. $200 at 5% for 4 periods _____

MODULE 3 UNIT 10

N-CHART

THE PRESENT VALUE OF MONEY

Lost Investment Opportunities
Present Value of $1 after "n" Periods

Periods (in years)	1%	2%	3%	4%	5%	6%	7%	8%	9%	10%	11%	12%
1	.99010	.98039	.97087	.96154	.96238	.94340	.93458	.92593	.91743	.90909	.90090	.89286
2	.98030	.96117	.94260	.92456*	.90793	.89000	.87344	.85734	.84168	.82645	.81162	.79719
3	.97059	.94232	.91514	.88900	.86384	.83962	.81630	.79383	.77218	.75131	.73119	.71178
4	.96098	.92385	.88849	.85480	.82379	.79209	.76290	.73503	.70843	.68301	.65873	.63552
5	.95147	.90573	.86261	.82193	.70363	.74726	.71299	.68058	.64993	.62092	.59345	.56743
6	.94204	.88797	.83748	.79031	.74622	.70496	.66634	.63017	.59627	.56447	.53464	.50663
7	.93272	.87056	.81309	.75992	.71068	.66506	.62275	.58349	.54703	.51316	.48166	.45235
8	.92348	.85349	.78941	.73069	.67404	.62741	.58201	.54027	.50187	.46651	.43393	.40388
9	.91434	.83675	.76642	.70259	.64461	.59190	.54393	.50025	.46043	.42410	.39092	.36061
10	.90529	.82035	.74409	.67556	.61391	.56839	.50835	.46319	.42241	.38554	.35218	.32197
11	.89632	.80426	.72242	.64958	.58468	.52679	.47509	.42888	.38753	.35049	.31728	.28748
12	.88745	.78849	.70138	.62440	.56684	.49697	.44401	.39711	.35553	.31683	.28584	.25667
13	.87866	.77303	.68095	.60057	.53932	.46884	.41496	.36770	.32618	.28966	.25751	.22917
14	.86996	.75787	.66112	.57747	.50607	.44230	.38782	.34046	.29925	.26333	.23199	.20462
15	.86135	.74301	.64186	.55526	.48102	.41726	.36245	.31524	.27454	.23939	.20900	.18270

To find the present value, take a given interest rate, go down column to correct number of periods, then multiply by the number you find.

*If it will be two years before you receive the dollar, and you could have invested it at 4%, you are actually receiving 92 cents.

CHAPTER 48 INVESTMENT GOALS AND RISK TOLERANCE

N-CHART

THE FUTURE VALUE OF MONEY

Future Value of $1 after "n" Periods

Periods (in years)	1%	2%	3%	4%	5%	6%	7%	8%	9%	10%	11%	12%
1	1.0100	1.0200	1.0300	1.0400	1.0500	1.0600	1.0700	1.0800	1.0900	1.1000	1.1100	1.1200
2	1.0201	1.0404	1.0609	1.0816*	1.1025	1.1236	1.1449	1.1664	1.1881	1.2100	1.2321	1.2544
3	1.0303	1.0612	1.0927	1.1249	1.1576	1.1910	1.2250	1.2597	1.2950	1.3310	1.3676	1.4049
4	1.0406	1.0824	1.1255	1.1699	1.2155	1.2625	1.3108	1.3605	1.4116	1.4641	1.5181	1.5735
5	1.0510	1.1041	1.1593	1.2167	1.2763	1.3382	1.4026	1.4693	1.5386	1.6105	1.6851	1.7623
6	1.0615	1.1261	1.1941	1.2653	1.3401	1.4185	1.5007	1.5869	1.6771	1.7716	1.8704	1.9738
7	1.0721	1.1487	1.2299	1.3159	1.4071	1.5036	1.6058	1.7138	1.8280	1.9487	2.0762	2.2107
8	1.0829	1.1717	1.2668	1.3686	1.4775	1.5939	1.7182	1.8509	1.9926	2.1436	2.3045	2.4760
9	1.0937	1.1951	1.3048	1.4233	1.5513	1.6895	1.8385	1.9990	2.1719	2.3580	2.5580	2.7731
10	1.1046	1.2190	1.3439	1.4802	1.6209	1.7909	1.9672	2.1589	2.3674	2.5937	2.8394	3.1059
11	1.1157	1.2434	1.3842	1.5395	1.7103	1.8983	2.1049	2.3316	2.5084	2.8531	3.1518	3.4786
12	1.1268	1.2682	1.4258	1.6010	1.7959	2.0122	2.2522	2.5182	2.8127	3.1384	2.4985	3.8960
13	1.1381	1.2936	1.4685	1.6651	1.8057	2.1329	2.4098	2.7196	3.0658	3.4523	3.8833	4.3635
14	1.1495	1.3195	1.5126	1.7317	1.9799	2.2609	2.5785	2.9372	3.3417	3.7975	4.3104	4.8871
15	1.1610	1.3459	1.5580	1.8009	2.0789	2.3966	2.7590	3.1722	3.6425	4.1773	4.7846	5.4736

To find the future value, take a given interest rate, go down column to correct number of periods, then multiply by the number you find.

* If you invest $1 at 4% for two years, it will be worth $1.08 at the end of that period.

CHAPTER 49

INVESTING FOR A SECURE FUTURE

CRITICAL THINKING ABOUT... INVESTING

1. Pretend you have $10,000 to invest. How would you choose to invest it? From the possibilities below, decide how much you would put into each investment. In other words, how would you diversify? Create your own portfolio, but remember, the total has to add up to $10,000.

   - Savings account (historically, two to three percent ROI): $_____

   - "Blue Chip" stock (a high-quality stock with an ROI of ten percent over the last ten years): $_____

   - New computer company's stock (ROI over the last six months of 25%): $_____

   - Mutual fund that invests in a wide variety of stocks (ROI over last ten years of 11%): $_____

   - S&P Index mutual fund (ROI over last ten years of 11%): $_____

   - Bonds that pay six percent interest and return the principal after 20 years: $_____

   - *Total invested:* $_____

2. Describe your portfolio.

   _____
   _____
   _____
   _____
   _____
   _____
   _____
   _____
   _____

CHAPTER 49 INVESTING FOR A SECURE FUTURE

3. Choose imaginary sums that you would invest in this portfolio each year:

    $_____ in stocks; $_____ in bonds; $_____ in cash

4. Rebalancing: I will rebalance my portfolio once a year on (date):
    _____

5. Calculate the value of your portfolio 20 years from now without further investment. To do this you will need to create a *weighted* (average) ROI for your portfolio, because each segment may have a different ROI.

    (ROI on Investment A × Weight of Investment A)
    + (ROI on Investment B × Weight of Investment B)
    + (ROI on Investment C × Weight of Investment C)
    = Weighted Average ROI of All Investments

    For an example, see your textbook, pages 552-553.

    To find the future value of your portfolio, look up your weighted average return in the Future Value N-Chart on page 340 of the Workbook.
    _____
    _____
    _____
    _____

KEY CONCEPTS

1. Use the Future Value of an Annuity chart on the next page to figure the future value of the amount you plan to invest each year.
    _____
    _____
    _____

2. Figure the total future value of your portfolio by calculating the future value of the annuity.
    _____
    _____
    _____

FUTURE VALUE OF AN ANNUITY

n / i	3%	5%	7%	10%	12%	15%	20%
1	1.0000	1.0000	1.0000	1.0000	1.0000	1.0000	1.0000
2	2.0300	2.0500	2.0700	2.1000	2.1200	2.1500	2.2000
3	3.0909	3.1525	3.2149	3.3100	3.3744	3.4725	3.6400
4	4.1836	4.3101	4.4399	4.6410	4.7793	4.9934	5.3680
5	5.3091	5.5256	5.7507	6.1051	6.3528	6.7424	7.4416
10	11.4639	12.5779	13.8164	15.9374	17.5487	20.3037	25.9587
15	18.5989	21.5786	25.1290	31.7725	37.2797	47.5804	72.0351
20	26.8704	33.0660	40.9955	57.2750	72.0524	102.4436	186.6880
25	36.4593	47.7271	63.2490	98.3471	133.3339	212.7930	471.9811
30	47.5754	66.4388	94.4608	164.4940	241.3327	434.7451	1181.8816
40	75.4013	120.7998	199.6351	442.5926	1358.2300	1779.0903	7343.8578
50	112.7969	209.3480	406.5289	1163.9085	2400.0182	7217.7163	45497.1908

CHAPTER 49 INVESTING FOR A SECURE FUTURE

VOCABULARY

Choose the best definition from each set of answers. Circle your answers.

1. annuity
    a. a sum of money that is paid or invested annually
    b. payment received for lending money
    c. the future value of an investment

2. portfolio
    a. a collection of stocks
    b. a collection of business documents
    c. a collection of investments

CHAPTER 49 QUIZ
Investing for a Secure Future

1. Draw a pie chart depicting an appropriate portfolio balance for an investor with a low risk tolerance who wants to pay for college in five years.

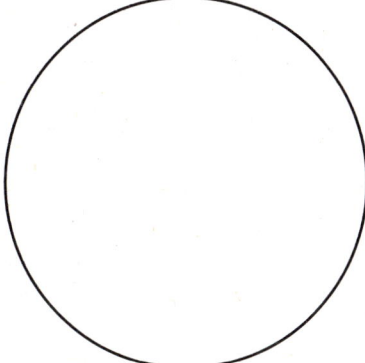

2. Draw a pie chart depicting an appropriate portfolio balance for an investor with a medium risk tolerance who wants to invest for retirement in 25 years.

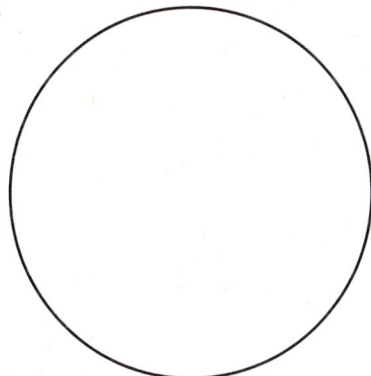

3. Draw a pie chart depicting an appropriate portfolio balance for an investor with a high risk tolerance who wants to buy a house in 12 years.

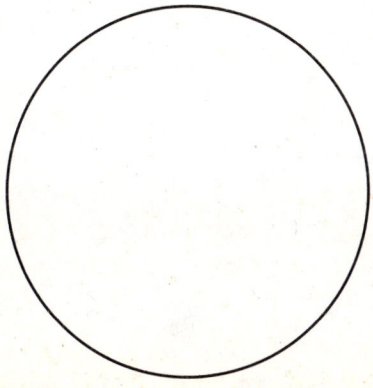

CHAPTER 49 INVESTING FOR A SECURE FUTURE

4. What is a good reason to balance your portfolio?
_____
_____
_____

Using the table on page 343, calculate the future value of the following annuities:

5. $3,000 for 20 years at 10%
_____

6. $10,000 for 5 years at 7%
_____

7. $300 for 40 years at 12%
_____

EXIT STRATEGIES:
Creating Wealth

CRITICAL THINKING ABOUT... EXIT STRATEGIES

1. How is harvesting different from replication?

2. Describe your hopes for the growth of your business. How much wealth do you imagine you could receive from eventually exiting your business? Why? Imagine you could earn $1 million ten years from now by selling your company. What would you do with the money?

3. About how much money do you expect your business to earn each year? Given this potential, approximately how much do you think your business will be worth after five years?

CHAPTER 50 EXIT STRATEGIES: Creating Wealth

4. Choose the exit strategy that you will include in your business plan. Write a short paragraph explaining this strategy to your investors.

___
___
___
___
___
___
___
___
___
___
___
___

KEY CONCEPTS

1. A rule of thumb is that a business can be sold for about three times its net annual profit. Using that rule, fill in the chart below for the following businesses.

Business	Average Yearly Profit	Estimated Sale Price
Web-site design	$4,000	$ _____
Aquarium cleaning	$1,000	$ _____
DJ service	$7,500	$ _____
Clothing boutique	$30,000	$ _____

2. Describe some of the investors you either have, or hope to have, for your company. What kind of exit strategy do you think would appeal to them most? Explain.

___
___
___
___
___
___

MODULE 3 UNIT 10

3. Choose an entrepreneur you admire who became wealthy, and answer the following questions (research on the Internet may help). Use separate paper if you need more space.

- How did this entrepreneur gain his or her wealth?
- What has he or she done with it?
- Why do you admire this individual?

VOCABULARY

Write a paragraph explaining your strategies for exiting your business in the future. Use all of the vocabulary words.

exit strategy ■ harvesting ■ liquidation ■ merger ■ net present value

CHAPTER 50 QUIZ

Exit Strategies: Creating Wealth

1. What is an "exit strategy"?
   _____
   _____
   _____

2. List three harvesting strategies.

   a. _____

   b. _____

   c. _____

3. Why is harvesting better than liquidation?
   _____
   _____
   _____
   _____

4. If you were to sell your business, would you prefer a merger/acquisition, management buyout, or employee stock ownership plan, and why?
   _____
   _____
   _____
   _____
   _____

5. Why is an exit strategy also important to your current investors?
   _____
   _____
   _____
   _____

Advanced Module
Business Plan Review

It is necessary to try to surpass oneself always; this occupation ought to last as long as life.
— Queen Christina of Sweden *(1626-1689)*

Congratulations! If you've made it this far, you have given yourself a thorough entrepreneurial education. You are ready to write a business plan that will impress potential investors and lenders.

If you are satisfied with your Intermediate Business Plan, use those worksheets to help you fill out your Advanced Business Plan. This is an opportunity, however, to improve on your Intermediate Business Plan or even change it entirely. In addition, this Advanced Business Plan includes a projected balance sheet, financing strategy, and exit strategy planning. These features will make your plan a better road map for you to use to run your business, and will make it more attractive to investors.

Before showing a business plan to investors, you may want to hire experts to help you tweak sections. An accountant can help make sure your financial statements are correct, for example.

Give detailed answers to the following business plan review questions. Use separate paper if you need additional space for your answers.

ADVANCED MODULE: BUSINESS PLAN REVIEW

Raising Capital (Chapter 31)

1. Describe financing sources that might be willing to invest in your business in exchange for equity.

   Friends and family: _____

   "Angels": _____

   MESBICs: _____

2. What other financing sources would be willing to invest in your business in exchange for equity?

   _____
   _____
   _____

Corporations (Chapter 32)

1. Is your business a: C Corporation _____

   Subchapter-S _____

   Limited Liability Company (LLC) _____

   Nonprofit Corporation _____

2. Why did you choose this corporate structure?

   _____
   _____
   _____
   _____

3. Who are the stockholders of your corporation?

   _____
   _____
   _____
   _____

ADVANCED MODULE: BUSINESS PLAN REVIEW

4. Who is on your board of directors?

   _____
   _____
   _____
   _____
   _____
   _____

Stocks (Chapter 33)

1. If your business is incorporated, describe what percentage of your company is represented by one share of stock.

   _____
   _____
   _____
   _____

2. Is your corporation's stock publicly or privately held?

   _____
   _____
   _____
   _____

Bonds (Chapter 34)

1. Do you intend to use debt to finance your business? Explain.

   _____
   _____
   _____
   _____
   _____

ADVANCED MODULE: BUSINESS PLAN REVIEW

2. Would you ever issue bonds to finance your business?
   _____
   _____
   _____

Your Balance Sheet (Chapter 35)

1. Create a Projected Balance Sheet for your business for one year.

BALANCE SHEET	
Assets	**Liabilities**
Cash: $ _____	Short-Term Liabilities: $ _____
Inventory: _____	Long-Term Liabilities: _____
Capital Equipment: _____	
Other Assets: _____	Owner's Equity: $ _____
Total Assets: $ _____	**Total Liabilities + OE:** $ _____

2. Create a pie chart showing your assets, short-term liabilities, long-term liabilities, and owner's equity.

3. What is your debt ratio?
   _____
   _____
   _____

ADVANCED MODULE: BUSINESS PLAN REVIEW

4. What is your debt-to-equity ratio?

Venture Capital (Chapter 36)

Have you found any sources of venture capital that you intend to contact? Describe.

Contracts (Chapter 37)

1. What is the most important contract you will need to run your business?

2. Describe any additional contracts you have, or plan to secure.

3. Who is your attorney?

ADVANCED MODULE: BUSINESS PLAN REVIEW

Socially Responsible Business (Chapter 38)

1. Choose three of the ways below you would use to run a socially responsible business.

   Recycling paper, glass, and plastic.   _____

   Donating a portion of profits to a nonprofit.   _____

   Not using animals to test products.   _____

   Offering employees incentives to volunteer in the community.   _____

   Establishing a safe and healthy workplace.   _____

   Other. _____
   _____
   _____

2. What cause-related marketing do you intend to use? How will this support and reinforce your competitive advantage?
   _____
   _____
   _____
   _____
   _____
   _____
   _____

Small Business and Government (Chapter 39)

What laws — such as minimum wage and age requirements, health and safety regulations, or anti-discrimination laws — will affect your business?
_____
_____
_____
_____
_____
_____

ADVANCED MODULE: BUSINESS PLAN REVIEW

Building Good Personal and Business Credit (Chapter 40)

1. My *personal* credit history is:

   Bad _____

   Good _____

   Not yet established _____

   Describe how you plan to establish good personal credit.

   _____
   _____
   _____
   _____

2. My *business* credit history is:

   Bad _____

   Good _____

   Not yet established _____

   Describe how you plan to establish good business credit.

   _____
   _____
   _____
   _____

Cash Flow (Chapter 41)

1. Use the cash flow chart on the next page to create a projected cash flow statement for your business for one year.

2. Calculate the "burn rate" for your business.

   _____
   _____
   _____

ADVANCED MODULE: BUSINESS PLAN REVIEW

NFTE CASH FLOW STATEMENT

Business: _____ **Date:** _____

Beginning Cash Balance: _____ $ _____

    Cash Inflow

        Investment: $ _____

        Sales: _____

    Total Cash Inflow: $ _____

    Cash Outflow

        Inventory: $ _____

        Variable Costs: _____

        Fixed Costs: _____

        Equipment: _____

        Other Outflows: _____

    Total Cash Outflow: $ _____ _____

Net Cash Flow: _____

Ending Cash Balance: $ _____

---

3. Use your projected balance sheet (Chapter 35) to calculate your working capital.

_____
_____
_____
_____

Intellectual Property (Chapter 42)

1. Describe any intellectual property you are developing for your business.

_____
_____
_____
_____

2. How do you intend to protect your intellectual property? Explain why it qualifies for this protection.

Ethical Business Behavior (Chapter 43)

1. Describe the corporate governance plan for your business. It should include five policies (rules) that will be the backbone of your company's ethics.

2. Provide information on each of your mentors or advisors. If there will be a board of advisors, list each member and describe his or her commitment to the business.

ADVANCED MODULE: BUSINESS PLAN REVIEW

Taxation (Chapter 44)

Which tax forms will you have to fill out for your business? Check all that apply.

    1040 U.S. Individual Tax Return   _____

    Schedule C, Profit or Loss from Business   _____

    Schedule SE, Self-Employment Tax   _____

    Quarterly Sales and Use Tax Return   _____

Insurance (Chapter 45)

1. What types of insurance will your business need? Explain.

   _____

   _____

   _____

   _____

2. Describe the premium, deductible, and payout for each policy you plan to carry.

   _____

   _____

   _____

   _____

Franchising and Licensing (Chapter 46)

Do you plan to franchise your business, or license any of your products? Explain.

_____

_____

_____

_____

ADVANCED MODULE: BUSINESS PLAN REVIEW

International Opportunities (Chapter 47)

1. Are there customers for your business in other countries? How do you plan to reach them?

   _____
   _____
   _____
   _____

2. Describe any international competitors you have found who may be able to access your customers. How do you intend to compete?

   _____
   _____
   _____
   _____
   _____
   _____
   _____
   _____

Investment Goals and Risk Tolerance (Chapter 48)

1. I plan to save _____ % of my net income to achieve personal financial goals.

2. My primary financial goal is _____.

3. My investment risk tolerance is _____.

Investing for a Secure Future (Chapter 49)

1. I will invest my savings as follows:

   Current Cash Value   **Investment Mix**

   Stocks $ _____   Stocks   _____ %

   Bonds $ _____   Bonds   _____ %

   Cash $ _____   Cash   _____ %

ADVANCED MODULE: BUSINESS PLAN REVIEW

2. My weighted average ROI is: _____
   _____
   _____
   _____

3. Using the Rule of 72, the number of years it will take my portfolio to double is: _____ years.
   _____
   _____

Exit Strategy (Chapter 50)

1. Describe your exit strategy.
   _____
   _____
   _____
   _____
   _____
   _____
   _____
   _____
   _____

2. Why will this exit strategy be attractive to potential investors?
   _____
   _____
   _____
   _____
   _____
   _____

Sample Student Business Plans

The following sample business plans (covering the Basic and Intermediate chapters) are for real student businesses. You can use them as a guide while you develop your own business plan. Additionally, the Advanced Sample Student Business Plan appears in Appendix D of your textbook (pages 586-612). Review the business owners' answers in these plans, and note how they have created a road map to follow in running their businesses. After reading these sample business plans, consider how you could improve on your own business plan.

Basic Sample Student Business Plan (Chapters 1-16):
School Supply Solutions 364

Intermediate Sample Student Business Plan (Chapters 1-30):
Happy Paws Dog Walking Service 376

Advanced Sample Student Business Plan (Chapters 1-50):
Teen Greetings (pages 586-612 of the student textbook)

SCHOOL SUPPLY SOLUTIONS
Basic Sample Student Business Plan (Chapters 1-16)

Your Business Idea (Chapter 1)

1. Describe your business idea.

   I would like to sell pens, pencils, erasers, notebooks, and other kinds of school supplies to my classmates at Wingate High School in Williamsburg, Brooklyn.

2. What is the name of your business?

   School Supply Solutions

3. Explain how your idea will satisfy a consumer need.

   Students are busy and on the go. Sometimes they don't have the things they need for class — such as pencils or notebooks. Maybe they left a book bag at home or a pen ran out of ink. School Supply Solutions will be there to help them when this happens.

4. Provide contact information for each owner.

   Lisa Johnson, President and Owner

5. If there is more than one owner, describe how the business ownership will be shared.

   I do not plan to share ownership.

Economics of One Unit (Chapter 2)

1. Do you intend to pay yourself a salary, wage, dividend, or commission? Explain.

   I plan to pay myself in two different ways. Each month, I will earn a salary of $25. I also plan to pay myself a commission. For every transaction I make, I will pay myself 10% of the selling price as a "perk" (commission) to reward myself for making a successful sale.

2. What type of business are you starting?

   School Supply Solutions will be a retail business.

3. Calculate the Economics of One Unit for your business.

   My business will sell different products, such as pens, notebooks, pocket calculators, erasers. I plan to add new products if I see that there is a need for them. While some products will cost more than others, I am assuming that, on average, School Supply Solutions will earn $2.00 per sale. My business will use "keystoning" as a pricing strategy, so for every $1.00 I pay in COGS, my customers will pay twice that amount.

BASIC SAMPLE STUDENT BUSINESS PLAN: SCHOOL SUPPLY SOLUTIONS

ECONOMICS OF ONE UNIT (EOU)			
Retail Business: average unit of sale = $2.00			
Selling Price per Unit:			$2.00
Cost of Goods Sold per Unit:		$1.00	
Sales Commission @10%:	$0.20		
Total Other Variable Costs per Unit:	$0.20	0.20	
Total Variable Costs per Unit:		$1.20	1.20
Gross Profit per Unit:			$0.80

Return on Investment (Chapter 3)

Business Goals:

1. What is your short-term business goal (less than one year)? What do you plan to invest to achieve this goal? What is your expected ROI?

   My short-term goals are to:
   - Operate my business during my senior year of high school.
   - Generate $600 in sales within the first three months.
   - Use a portion of my net profit to pay for my senior prom and school activities.

2. What is your long-term business goal (from one to five years)? What do you plan to invest to achieve this goal? What is your expected ROI?

   My longer-term goals are to:
   - Operate my business when I am in college.
   - Use a portion of my net profit to buy a used car.
   - Generate $8,000 in sales by the end of my third year of operations.

Personal Goals:

1. What are your long-term personal and career goals?

   Career Goals:
   - Become an international business lawyer
   - Live and work overseas
   - Run my own law firm

BASIC SAMPLE STUDENT BUSINESS PLAN: SCHOOL SUPPLY SOLUTIONS

Life Goals:
- Learn to speak another language fluently
- Travel around the world
- Use my skills to help others

2. How much education will you need for your career?
   - High School Diploma
   - College Degree (BA)
   - Law Degree (JD)
   - Master's Degree in Business Administration (MBA)

3. Have you tried to get a part-time job related to your chosen career?

   Last summer I worked part-time at a law firm in New York City.

Opportunity Recognition (Chapter 4)

1. What resources and skills do you (and the other owners of your business) have that will help make your business successful?

   I am very outgoing and have been told that I am a good listener. I think that being successful in sales requires both of these skills. Even more importantly, I stick with things, even in the face of obstacles. I refuse to give up on a goal until I achieve it.

2. Perform a SWOT analysis of your business.

   Strengths (Entrepreneur's abilities and contacts)

   My customers will be my classmates, and these people are also my friends. I understand their needs and preferences. My customers trust me.

   Weaknesses (The problems the entrepreneur faces, from lack of money or training to lack of time or experience.)

   I will not have a fixed location for my business. This could make it difficult to connect with customers since they will not always be able to find me. To take care of this, I plan to use a cell phone for my business and include the number on all my promotional material.

   Opportunities (Lucky breaks or creative advantages the entrepreneur can use to get ahead of the competition.)

   At school, no one else is selling the kinds of products I plan to provide. Students can't succeed without school supplies.

Threats (Anything that might be bad for the business, from competitors to legal problems.)

Once other people see what a good idea I have, they could try to copy me, and then my business would have competition. If this happened, I would need to figure out how to stay ahead of competitors.

Core Beliefs (Chapter 5)

1. Describe three core beliefs you will use in running your company.

    I believe in honesty, providing people with a quality product, and that businesses exist to solve other people's problems.

2. Choose a motto for your company. (You can select or adapt from the 50 positive quotes in Chapter 5, find one elsewhere, or make up your own.)

    "School Supply Solutions: We Supply You with the Tools for Success"

Supply and Demand (Chapter 6)

1. What factors will influence the demand for your product or service?

    Demand for my products will depend on how often students forget to bring their own supplies to school or run out of something, or discover that the supplies they have don't work properly.

2. What factors will influence the supply for your product or service?

    My supply will depend upon me. I need to make arrangements to purchase new inventory regularly. I also need to remember to bring my products to school. I plan to store my inventory in my locker.

Product Development (Chapter 7)

How do you plan to protect your product/trademark/logo? (Check one, and explain.)

_____	patent
__✔__	copyright
__✔__	trademark
_____	trade secret

Explain:

Once I design a logo for my business, I will get it trademarked. I plan to produce marketing brochures, and those will be copyrighted.

BASIC SAMPLE STUDENT BUSINESS PLAN: SCHOOL SUPPLY SOLUTIONS

Competitive Advantage (Chapter 8)

1. What is your competitive advantage?

Competitive Advantage	Yes/No	Description
Quality	No	
Price	Yes	My products sell for 10% less than those sold by my closest competitor - a stationery store three blocks from the school.
Location	Yes	My business offers students convenience. They can get the products they need for school without leaving the building.
Selection	No	I know what products my customers will want to buy because I need the same supplies that they do.
Service	No	
Speed	Yes	
Reputation	Yes	People will buy from me because they know and trust me.

2. Who are your primary competitors? Where are they located?

   Sunshine Cards and Gifts: 536 Metropolitan Avenue, Brooklyn, NY 11211

   All in the Cards: 305 Broadway, Brooklyn, NY 11211

3. How will your business help others? List all organizations to which you plan to contribute. (Your contribution may be time, money, your product, or something else.)

   I will be helping my classmates to succeed in school. Without the basic supplies - notebook, pen, and pencils - students can't take notes. And if they can't take notes then they won't do well on tests and their grades will go down. I plan to donate 5% of my net profit to a local homeless shelter.

Operating Costs (Chapter 9)

1. List and describe your monthly fixed costs.

Utilities:	$10.00
Salaries:	$25.00
Advertising: *(per month to print flyers and post them around school)*	$10.00
Insurance:	$30.00
Interest:	$0.00

Rent:	$0.00
Depreciation:	$10.00
Total Monthly Fixed Costs:	**$85.00**

2. List and describe your monthly variable costs.

   Monthly Variable Costs

Cost of Goods Sold per Unit	# of Units Sold for month of September	Total COGS
$1.00	200	$200.00

3. Re-calculate your economics of one unit, allocating as many variable costs as possible.

   Other Variable Costs

Commission	Total Sales Revenue	Total Commission
10%	$400.00	$40.00

   Total Monthly Variable Costs

Cost of Goods Sold per Unit	Commission	
$200.00 +	$40.00 =	$240.00

Marketing (Chapter 10)

1. Describe the Four P's for your business.

   Product — Why will your product meet a consumer need?

   Students need school supplies and they often forget to bring their own to school or they run out.

   Place — Where do you intend to sell your product?

   I will sell supplies from my locker before school and between classes. During lunch, I will sell in the cafeteria. This will be very convenient for my customers.

   Price — What price do you plan to sell your product for, and why?

   I plan to keystone, or double the price that I paid for the products. I need to make sure, though, that I get a good deal on the products I purchase. A lot of students don't have much spending money so I'll need to keep my prices low.

   Promotion — How do you plan to advertise and promote your product?

   Word of mouth will help me to promote School Supply Solutions. I will also put up flyers in the school hallways and in the cafeteria.

BASIC SAMPLE STUDENT BUSINESS PLAN: SCHOOL SUPPLY SOLUTIONS

2. Fill out a marketing plan for your business.

Methods	Description	Target Market	Amount to Be Spent
Brochures	Brochures will describe my products and include an order form.	Students and teachers	$10.00
Business Cards	Cards will feature my name, e-mail, phone number and slogan.	Students and teachers	$17.00
Flyers	Flyers will feature my business name, slogan, and contact information.	Students	$5.00
Promo Items	I will give out pencils, pens, and erasers with my business card the first week of each grading period.	Students	$0.50 per packet × 100 = $5.00
Special Events	Visibility at sports events, plays, assemblies and other events at my school.	Students, teachers, and parents	No additional cost
E-mail	My mailing list will allow me to notify customers about special events, sales, and promotions.	Students	No additional cost. My monthly Internet fee of $10.00 is already accounted for in my fixed costs.

3. Do you intend to publicize your philanthropy? Why or why not? If you do, explain how you will work your philanthropy into your marketing.

    I plan to inform customers through my promotional materials that 5% of my profits will go to the local homeless shelter.

Market Research (Chapter 11)

1. Describe your target market.

    My target market consists of:
    - 850 teenagers ages 14-18 who attend the High School for Enterprise and Technology in Williamsburg, Brooklyn.
    - Teachers who work at my school.

- Parents who attend special school events such as sports events and concerts.

Through my market research, I learned that on average, each student at my school spends $75 per year on supplies. This means that students at my school are investing a total of $63,750 into the school supplies market each and every year! My goal is to capture at least 5% market share or about $3,200.

2. Brainstorm five Market Research questions.
   1. What are your favorite school supply products?
   2. What kinds of school supplies do you buy the most (and least) frequently?
   3. How much do you spend on school supplies each year?
   4. Where do you buy your school supplies now?
   5. Are there school supplies that you like/need that are difficult to find? What are they?

Record Keeping (Chapter 12)

1. Describe your record-keeping system.
   - I will keep electronic records for my business on my computer.
   - My accounting system will be "cash-only."
   - I plan to file my receipts in a filing cabinet so that I will have records of my all my expenses.
   - Each day, I will fill in my electronic spreadsheet to track which products I have sold and in what quantities. This way, I can see how my business is progressing.

2. List all bank accounts you will open for your business.

   I already have a savings account for my own personal use. I plan to open a second savings account at the same bank so that I can keep my business income separate from my personal savings.

Projected Income Statement (Chapter 13)

1. Complete a monthly projected budget and one-year income statement for your business. See the following pages 372-373.

BASIC SAMPLE STUDENT BUSINESS PLAN: SCHOOL SUPPLY SOLUTIONS

MONTHLY INCOME STATEMENT

School Supply Solutions **Date:** September, 2007

	# of Units	Unit Price		
Revenue:	200	$2.00		$400.00
Cost of Goods Sold		$1.00	$200.00	
Other Variable Costs				
Commission @10%:		0.20	40.00	
Total Variable Costs:			$240.00	240.00
Gross Profit:				$160.00
Fixed Operating Costs				
Utilities:		$10.00		
Salaries:		25.00		
Advertising:		10.00		
Insurance:		30.00		
Interest:		0.00		
Rent:		0.00		
Depreciation:		10.00		
Total Fixed Operating Costs:		$85.00		85.00
Pre-Tax Profit:				$75.00
Taxes (estimated 20%):				15.00
Net Profit:				$60.00

YEARLY INCOME STATEMENT
(My business will operate for ten months of the year.)

School Supply Solutions **Date:** 2007

	# of Units	Unit Price		
Revenue:	2,000	$2.00		$4,000.00
Cost of Goods Sold		$1.00	$2,000.00	
Other Variable Costs				
Commission @10%:		0.20	400.00	
Total Variable Costs:			$2,400.00	2,400.00
Gross Profit:				$1,600.00

BASIC SAMPLE STUDENT BUSINESS PLAN: SCHOOL SUPPLY SOLUTIONS

YEARLY INCOME STATEMENT (con't)

School Supply Solutions   Date: 2007

	# of Units	Unit Price	
Revenue:	2,000	$2.00	$4,000.00
Gross Profit:			$1,600.00
Fixed Operating Costs			
Utilities:		$10.00	$100.00
Salaries:		25.00	250.00
Advertising:		10.00	100.00
Insurance:		30.00	300.00
Interest:		0.00	0.00
Rent:		0.00	0.00
Depreciation:		10.00	100.00
Total Fixed Operating Costs:		$85.00	$850.00 850.00
Pre-Tax Profit:			$750.00
Taxes (estimated 20%):			150.00
Net Profit:			$600.00

---

2. Use your projected one-year income statement to calculate:

   Projected ROI for one year: (Net Profit ÷ Start-up Investment × 100)
   $600 ÷ $1,555 × 100 = 39%

   Projected ROS for one year: (Net Profit ÷ Sales × 100)
   $600 ÷ $4,000 × 100 = 15%

   Please see the table on the following page to get the Start-Up Investment for the ROI equation.

Financing Strategy (Chapter 14)

1. What legal structure have you chosen for your business? Why?

   School Supply Solutions will operate as a sole proprietorship. I understand that incorporating has advantages because it protects the business owner from losing personal assets if the business is sued or goes bankrupt. However, my business (school supplies) is not likely to cause a customer harm so my liability risk is low. It is also expensive to incorporate and I cannot afford this cost right now.

BASIC SAMPLE STUDENT BUSINESS PLAN: SCHOOL SUPPLY SOLUTIONS

2. Make a detailed list of the items you will need to start your business. What is your total start-up investment?

Item	Quantity	Cost
Equipment:		
Used Computer	1	$500.00
Cell Phone	1	$80.00
Printer/Fax/Copier	1	$100.00
Beginning Inventory (First 1-2 months):		
Pocket Folders	25	@ .60 each = $15.00
Pencils	50	@ .03/each = $1.50
Gelly Roll® Pens	50	@ .75/each = $37.50
Large Spiral Notebooks	25	@ 1.00/each = $25.00
Small Spiral Notebooks	15	@ .50/each = $7.50
Erasers	20	@ .05/each = $1.00
Liquid Eraser	5	@ 1.50/each = $7.50
Looseleaf Paper Packets	3	@ 1.00/each = $3.00
Other Costs		
Flyers	100	@ .05/each = $5.00
Copyright and Trademark Costs		$500.00
Business Cards	200	$17.00
Cash reserve covering 3 months of fixed costs		$255.00 (3 × $85)
Total Start-Up Investment:		**$1,555.00**

3. List the sources of financing for your start-up investment. Identify whether each source is equity, debt, or a gift. Indicate the amount and type for each source.

   My start-up investment will come from my own personal savings.

4. What is your debt ratio? What is your debt-to-equity ratio?

   My debt ratio is 0. My debt to equity ratio is 0:100. In other words, I have 100% equity in my business and zero debt.

5. What is your payback period? In other words, how long will it take you to earn enough profit to cover start-up capital?

Total Start-Up Investment = $1,555

Monthly Net Profit = $60

1,555 ÷ 60 = 26

My payback period will be 26 months (a little over two years).

Negotiation (Chapter 15)

Describe any suppliers with whom you will have to negotiate.

Since I plan to buy all of my inventory from a local office supply outlet, I would like to negotiate with the store manager to see if I can qualify for a frequent shopper or volume discount. I plan to keep track of my spending at the store. This way I can prove what a good customer I am.

Buying Wholesale (Chapter 16)

1. Where will you purchase the products you plan to sell, or the products you plan to use to manufacture the products you will be selling?

    I will purchase my inventory from an office supply outlet in downtown Brooklyn. I will also research office supply catalogues to see if I can find better prices and new items to add to my product line.

2. Have you applied for a sales-tax ID number?

    I am in the process of completing the application.

HAPPY PAWS DOG WALKING SERVICES
Intermediate Sample Student Business Plan (Chapters 1-30)

Your Business Idea (Chapter 1)

1. Describe your business idea.

   My business idea is to start a dog walking service in my neighborhood in Detroit.

2. What is the name of your business?

   Happy Paws Dog Walking Service

3. Explain how your idea will satisfy a consumer need.

   Many dog owners cannot walk their dogs during the afternoon because they are at work. Some elderly people who live in my neighborhood are unable to walk their dogs because they are homebound.

4. Provide contact information for each owner.

   Darius Jones
   504 Victoria Park Drive West
   Detroit, Michigan 48215
   313-555-9193

5. If there is more than one owner, describe how the business ownership will be shared.

   I will be totally responsible for running the business. My brother Charles will be a silent partner. He has a 25% equity stake in Happy Paws. This means that he will earn 25% of Happy Paws' net profit.

Economics of One Unit (Chapter 2)

1. Do you intend to pay yourself a salary, wage, dividend, or commission? Explain.

   I plan to pay myself in three different ways:
   - I am valuing my hourly labor cost for dog walking at $10
   - I will pay myself a 5% commission based on my sales revenue.
   - Dividend: If my business is profitable, I will pay myself a year-end dividend of 30% of my net profit. I will invest the remainder in my business to help it grow.

2. What type of business are you starting?

   Happy Paws will be a service business.

3. Calculate the Economics of One Unit for your business.

INTERMEDIATE SAMPLE STUDENT BUSINESS PLAN: HAPPY PAWS DOG WALKING SERVICE

ECONOMICS OF ONE UNIT (EOU)			
Service Business: unit = One hour of dog walking (includes pickup and drop-off)			
Selling Price per Unit:			$15.00
Cost of Services Sold per Unit			
Direct Labor:	$10.00		
Supplies:	0.25		
Total Cost of Services Sold per Unit:	$10.25	$10.25	
Other Variable Costs per Unit			
Sales Commission @5%:	$0.75		
Total Other Variable Costs per Unit:	$0.75	0.75	
Total Variable Costs per Unit:		$11.00	11.00
Gross Profit per Unit:			$4.00

Return on Investment (Chapter 3)

Business Goals:

1. What is your short-term business goal (less than one year)? What do you plan to invest to achieve this goal?

   My short-term goals are to:
   - Service at least 15 satisfied customers.
   - Average three dog walks per week per customer.
   - Retain each customer for at least six months of service.

   Strategy:
   - Purchase advertising and post flyers in my neighborhood.
   - Offer an incentive plan to repeat customers. Buy 10 walks and get the 11th walk free!

2. What is your long-term business goal (from one to five years)? What do you plan to invest to achieve this goal?

   My longer-term goals are to:
   - Expand my business by hiring employees.

INTERMEDIATE SAMPLE STUDENT BUSINESS PLAN: HAPPY PAWS DOG WALKING SERVICE

- Develop partnerships with pet stores, dog groomers, and obedience trainers.
- Service 50-100 customers per month.

Strategy:

- Save my net profit so I can afford to hire employees.
- Build relationships with other pet stores, dog groomers, and obedience trainers.
- Deliver excellent dog walking services to my clients. If I provide quality, they will refer me to new customers and my business will grow.

Personal Goals:

1. What are your long-term career and personal goals?

   Career Goals:
   - Become a veterinarian
   - Own and operate an animal shelter for homeless pets

   Life Goals:
   - Learn how to scuba dive
   - Travel to the Galapagos Islands in the Pacific
   - Raise a family of my own
   - Own many pets!

2. How much education will you need for your career?
   - High School Diploma
   - College Degree (probably in Biology) (4 years)
   - Degree in Veterinary Medicine and Business (5 years)

3. Have you tried to get a part-time job related to your chosen career?

   During the summer months, I volunteer at a local horse stable where they have a veterinarian who works on staff. I have learned about the field from my conversations with her.

Opportunity Recognition (Chapter 4)

1. What resources and skills do you (and the other owners of your business) have that will help make your business successful?
   - I have grown up around animals and I love to take care of them.

- It is my hobby to read about different breeds of dogs. I am a walking encyclopedia about "man's best friend."
- Dog owners in my neighborhood know that I am a responsible pet owner and will trust me with their pets.

2. Perform a SWOT analysis of your business.

Strengths (Entrepreneur's abilities and contacts)

I am knowledgeable about dogs and enjoy being around them.

Weaknesses (The problems the entrepreneur faces, from lack of money or training to lack of time or experience.)

I do not have a car so for the time being it will be difficult for me to expand my business beyond my immediate neighborhood.

Opportunities (Lucky breaks or creative advantages the entrepreneur can use to get ahead of the competition.)

Many professionals are too busy to walk their dogs, and elderly dog owners have difficulty taking their dogs outside, especially during the winter months.

Threats (Anything that might be bad for the business, from competitors to legal problems.)

Other dog walking services exist in Detroit but none in my neighborhood. I plan to rely on a good reputation and affordable pricing to outperform the competition.

Core Beliefs (Chapter 5)

1. Describe three core beliefs you will use in running your company.
   - Happy Paws will treat all dogs with kindness and respect.
   - Happy Paws is not just a dog walking service; it is a business that values the unique relationship between pets and people.
   - Happy Paws believes in honesty and integrity. Happy Paws wants its customers to be happy, too.

2. Choose a motto for your company. (You can select or adapt from the 50 positive quotes in Chapter 5, find one elsewhere, or make up your own.)

"We take pride in being a dog's best friend."

INTERMEDIATE SAMPLE STUDENT BUSINESS PLAN: HAPPY PAWS DOG WALKING SERVICE

Supply and Demand (Chapter 6)

1. What factors will influence the demand for your product or service?

   Demand Factors:
   - How much free time my customers have - and what they choose to do with their free time.
   - The weather (I expect greater demand during the colder months).

2. What factors will influence the supply for your product or service?

   Supply Factors:
   - Time: I can only operate my business after school and on weekends.
   - Lack of Transportation: Not having a car limits the supply of my services. I will not be able to travel to different localities to deliver my services. My business will focus on my immediate neighborhood.

Product Development (Chapter 7)

How do you plan to protect your product/trademark/logo? (Check one, and explain.)

_____ patent
_____ copyright
__✔__ trademark
_____ trade secret

Explain:

I am developing a logo for my business. Once my logo is finished, I will get it trademarked.

Competitive Advantage (Chapter 8)

1. What is your competitive advantage?

   I have several competitive advantages:

Competitive Advantage	Yes/No	Description
Quality	Yes	Each dog will be walked for at least one hour. My competitors typically offer 30-45 minute walks.

INTERMEDIATE SAMPLE STUDENT BUSINESS PLAN: HAPPY PAWS DOG WALKING SERVICE

Competitive Advantage	Yes/No	Description
Price	Yes	My rates are lower than those offered by my closest competitors.
Location	No	
Selection	No	
Service	Yes	I will deliver a high quality, personalized service. Each dog will have its own file, and I will keep track of its unique features and needs.
Speed	No	
Reputation	Yes	Dog owners know that I am responsible and knowledgeable about pets. They have seen me walking my family's dogs for the last ten years.

2. Who are your primary competitors? Where are they located?

   There are approximately 25 dog-walking services currently operating in the greater Detroit area.

3. How will your business help others? List all organizations to which you plan to contribute. (Your contribution may be time, money, your product, or something else.)

   I plan to donate 5% of my yearly net profit to the ASPCA. I will also volunteer at my local animal shelter one Sunday each month.

Operating Costs (Chapter 9)

1. List and describe your monthly fixed costs.

   Utilities:

Internet:	$20.00
Cell Phone:	$30.00

   Salaries: *(I am valuing my contribution to the business as CEO/Owner at a monthly rate of $50.)* $50.00

Advertising:	$35.00
Insurance:	$40.00
Interest:	$0.00
Rent:	$0.00
Depreciation:	$5.00
Total Monthly Fixed Costs:	**$180.00**

2. List and describe your monthly variable costs.

Monthly Variable Costs

Cost of Services Sold per Unit	# of Units Sold per month	Total COSS
$10.25	150	$1,537.50

Direct Labor and Supplies: I value my direct labor for dog walking at an hourly rate of $10. My supplies will cost $0.25 per one-hour dog walk. I intend to walk dogs 150 hours per month. My monthly variable COSS will be $1,500.00.

Other Variable Costs

Commission	Total Sales Revenue	Total Commission
5%	$2,250.00	$112.50

Commission: I will allocate 5% of my total sales revenue as a commission.
On average, I plan to generate $2,250 in sales per month. My monthly commission would then be $112.50.

Total Monthly Variable Costs

Cost of Services Sold per Unit	Commission	
$1,500.00 +	$112.50 =	$1,612.50

Marketing (Chapter 10)

1. Describe the Four P's for your business.

   Product or Service — Why will your product meet a consumer need?
   - Many people are not able to walk their dogs during the afternoon.
   - Elderly people are physically limited and may not be able to walk their dogs even though they have the time to do so.

   Place — Where do you intend to sell your product?
   - Happy Paws is a service business so I will bring my services directly to the customer. I will pick up each dog from its home.

   Price — What price do you plan to sell your product for, and why?
   - Customers will be charged a "dog walk" fee of $15 per walk. This will include the time required to pick up and drop off each pet. Dogs will be walked for at least 60 minutes.

   Promotion — How do you plan to advertise and promote your product?
   - Flyers
   - Monthly classified ad in my local newspaper
   - Word of mouth

2. Fill out a marketing plan for your business.

Methods	Description	Target Market	Amount to Be Spent
Business Cards	Business cards with my name, e-mail, phone number and slogan.	Dog owners	$17.00
Flyers	I will create and post flyers for my business at pet stores, local supermarkets, and the nearest animal clinic.	Dog owners	$5.00
Special Events	I plan to promote my business at special events in my neighborhood, such as block parties and at our annual Halloween festival. I will give away free candy and dog treats to attract customers.	Dog owners	$5-$10 for candy and dog treats.
E-mail	I will create a mailing list so that I can stay in touch with my customers and inform them about special dog care tips.	Dog owners	No additional cost. My monthly Internet fee of $10 is already accounted for in my fixed costs.

3. Do you intend to publicize your philanthropy? Why or why not? If you do, explain how you will work your philanthropy into your marketing.

Yes. I think it is important for my customers to know how committed I am to animal care. By supporting my business, they will also be supporting our local ASPCA.

Market Research (Chapter 11)

1. Research your industry and display the results in a report that includes pie charts and bar or line graphs. Describe your target market within the industry.

In doing research online, I have learned that there are at least 25 dog walking services in Detroit. Half of the competitors I researched offer pet "day care," long-term kenneling, and obedience training in addition to dog walking. I am planning to stay focused on dog walking only. I also learned that pet ownership is increasing in Detroit.

In 2000, 13% of all households owned pets. By 2004, this increased to 15%.

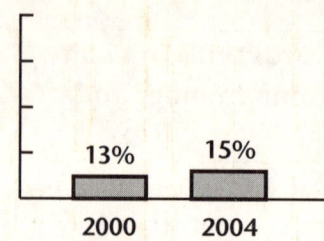

% of Detroit Households with Pets

2. Describe your market segment and the results of your research on this market segment.

   My target market consists of:

   - Busy professionals, ages 30-50:
     - 50% are married
     - Of those that are married, 30% have small children
     - Enjoy spending free time outside the home
     - Annual income averages $60,000
   - Homebound elderly dog owners, ages 70-90:
     - Physically unable to walk their dogs
     - Fixed income of $40,000 on average
     - They love their pets and want to take good care of them.

Record Keeping (Chapter 12)

1. Describe your record-keeping system.

   I will keep customer billing and dog-characteristic records in electronic spreadsheets. Every customer will also have a separate paper file. These files will include information about each pet, such as age, breed, and special health or behavioral issues. I will bill my customers each month.

2. List all bank accounts you will open for your business.

   I already have a savings and checking account. I will open a second savings account for business deposits only.

Projected Income Statement (Chapter 13)

1. Complete a monthly projected budget and one-year income statement for your business.

INTERMEDIATE SAMPLE STUDENT BUSINESS PLAN: HAPPY PAWS DOG WALKING SERVICE

MONTHLY INCOME STATEMENT

Happy Paws **Date:** September, 2007

	# of Units	Unit Price	
Revenue:	150	$15.00	$2,250.00
Cost of Services Sold			
Direct Labor:		$10.00	$1,500.00
Supplies:		0.25	37.50
Other Variable Costs			
Commission @5%:		0.75	112.50
Total Variable Costs:		$11.00	$1,650.00	1,650.00
Gross Profit:			**$600.00**
Fixed Operating Costs			
Utilities:		$50.00	
Salaries:		50.00	
Advertising:		35.00	
Insurance:		40.00	
Interest:		0.00	
Rent:		0.00	
Depreciation:		5.00	
Total Fixed Operating Costs:		$180.00	180.00
Pre-Tax Profit:			**$420.00**
Taxes (estimated 20%):			84.00
Net Profit:			**$336.00**

See the Yearly Income Statement on the following page.

2. Use your projected one-year income statement to calculate:

   Projected ROI for one year: (Net Profit ÷ Start-up Investment × 100)
   $4,032 ÷ $1,260 × 100 = 320%

   Projected ROS for one year: (Net Profit ÷ Sales × 100)
   $4,032 ÷ $27,000 × 100 = 14.9%

   Please see the table on page 387 to get the Start-Up Investment for the ROI equation.

INTERMEDIATE SAMPLE STUDENT BUSINESS PLAN: HAPPY PAWS DOG WALKING SERVICE

YEARLY INCOME STATEMENT

Happy Paws   Date: 2007

	# of Units	Unit Price		
Revenue:	1,800	$15.00		$27,000.00
Cost of Services Sold				
Direct Labor:		$10.00	$18,000.00	
Supplies:		0.25	450.00	
Other Variable Costs				
Commission @5%:		0.75	1,350.00	
Total Variable Costs:		$11.00	$19,800.00	19,800.00
Gross Profit:				**$7,200.00**
Fixed Operating Costs				
Utilities:		$50.00	$600.00	
Salaries:		50.00	600.00	
Advertising:		35.00	420.00	
Insurance:		40.00	480.00	
Interest:		0.00	0.00	
Rent:		0.00	0.00	
Depreciation:		5.00	60.00	
Total Fixed Operating Costs:		$180.00	$2,160.00	2,160.00
Pre-Tax Profit:				**$5,040.00**
Taxes (estimated 20%):				1,008.00
Net Profit:				**$4,032.00**

Darius's Profit (75% equity stake) = $3,024.00

Darius's Brother's Profit (25% equity stake) = $1,008.00

Financing Strategy (Chapter 14)

1. What legal structure have you chosen for your business? Why?

    Happy Paws will be a sole proprietorship. At this time, my business is just beginning and I am the only employee. However, as my business grows, I would like to change my legal structure so that I am incorporated as a Subchapter-S Corp. This way, if I am ever sued, my personal savings and other assets will be protected.

INTERMEDIATE SAMPLE STUDENT BUSINESS PLAN: HAPPY PAWS DOG WALKING SERVICE

2. List the cost of the items you will need to buy to start your business.

Item	Quantity	Cost		
Equipment:				
Cell Phone	1	$60.00		
Printer	1	$100.00		
Beginning Inventory (First 1-2 months):				
Plastic Bags	1 box (contains 1,000 bags)	@ $10.00 each =	$10.00	
Extra Leashes	5	@ $15.00 each =	$75.00	
Dog Treats	2 bags	@ $7.50 each =	$15.00	
Dog Toys	Assortment of 5	@ $3.00 each =	$15.00	
Hanging File Folders	1 packet	@ $4.00 each =	$4.00	
Manila File Folders	1 packet	@ $2.00 each =	$2.00	
Other Costs				
Trademarking Fee		$350.00		
Flyers	100	@ $0.05 each =	$5.00	
Business Cards	200	$14.00		
Advertising	2 classified ads	$70.00		
Cash reserve covering 3 months of fixed costs		$540.00 (3 × $180)		
Total Start-Up Investment:		$1,260.00		

3. List the sources of financing for your start-up investment. Identify whether each source is equity, debt, or a gift. Indicate the amount and type for each source.

Funding Source	Equity	Debt	Gift
Personal Savings	$500.00 (75% equity)		
Charles Jones (brother)	$250.00 (25% equity)		
Stephanie Jones (mother)			$510.00
Subtotal	$750.00	$0	$510.00

TOTAL START-UP INVESTMENT = $1,260.00

4. What is your debt ratio? What is your debt-to-equity ratio?

My debt ratio is zero because I will have no debt when I start Happy Paws. My debt-to-equity ratio will be 0:75. I will have 75% equity in Happy Paws. My brother Charles will hold the remaining 25% in equity.

5. What is your payback period? In other words, how long will it take you to earn enough profit to cover start-up capital?

   Total Start-Up Investment = $1,260

   Monthly Net Profit = $336

   1,260 ÷ 336 = 3.75

   My payback period will be 3.75 months.

Negotiation (Chapter 15)

Describe any suppliers with whom you will have to negotiate.

My business does not require me to purchase many products. From time to time I will buy doggie treats and dog toys.

Buying Wholesale (Chapter 16)

1. Where will you purchase the products you plan to sell, or the products you plan to use to manufacture the products you will be selling?

Item	Location
Dog treats, toys, and pet supplies	Sunshine Pet Emporium
File folders and office supplies	Bob's Office Supplies
Plastic bags	Key Food Mart

2. Have you applied for a sales-tax ID number?

   I am in the process of completing the application.

Your Competitive Strategy (Chapter 17)

1. Use the following charts to define your business, analyze your competitive advantage, and determine your tactics.

Business Definition Question	Response
1. *The Offer:* What products and services will be sold by the business? 2. *Target Market:* Which consumer segment will the business focus on?	1. Happy Paws is a dog walking service. 2. Happy Paws' primary consumer segments: busy professionals and homebound elderly dog owners.

INTERMEDIATE SAMPLE STUDENT BUSINESS PLAN: HAPPY PAWS DOG WALKING SERVICE

Business Definition Question	Response
3. *Production Capability:* How will that offer be produced and delivered to those customers?	3. I will be delivering my dog walking service directly. I plan to go to customers' homes after school and on weekends for dog pickups and drop-offs.

Competitive Advantage Question	Competitive Difference (USP)
1. *The Offer:* What will be better or different about the products and services that will be sold by the business?	1. I plan to emphasize my extensive knowledge of dogs and pet care in all marketing materials.
2. *Target Market:* What customers should be the focus of the business, to make it as successful as possible?	2. I will focus on offering busy professionals and homebound elderly dog owners a reliable, quality, and affordable service.
3. *Production and Delivery Capability:* What will be better or different about the way that offer is produced and delivered to those customers?	3. My services will be less expensive than what my competition charges.

Tactical Question	Issue	Solution
1. *Sales Plan:* Where and how will you sell to your customers?	How to identify prospects and convert them to sales.	I will walk door to door in my neighborhood to pass out flyers and business cards. I also plan to advertise in my local paper.
2. *Market Communications:* How will you communicate with your customers and make them aware of your business offer?	How to make customers aware of your offer; how to attract them to the business.	I will send out press releases. I hope to get local newspapers to write about my business.
3. *Operating Plan:* How will you manage your internal operations?	How to make the business go, and determine who will perform the tasks.	In the beginning, I will be performing all of the tasks for Happy Paws — from dog walking to marketing to budgeting. I will invest two hours per week on operational tasks such as billing and keeping track of cash inflows and outflows.

INTERMEDIATE SAMPLE STUDENT BUSINESS PLAN: HAPPY PAWS DOG WALKING SERVICE

Tactical Question	Issue	Solution
4. *Budget:* How do you plan to manage your revenues and expenses?	What are the sources of revenue? What are the items that have to be purchased?	My revenue will come from billing customers for my dog walking services. I plan to bill on a monthly basis. I will keep track of the number of walks I have completed per dog and bill customers accordingly. I will purchase supplies in the middle of each month, after my revenue from the previous month is collected.

2. Describe your strategy for outperforming the competition.

   My strategy for beating my competitors is simple: provide a reliable, quality, and affordable service to dog owners in my neighborhood.

3. What tactics will you use to carry out this strategy?

   I plan to rely on word of mouth and referrals. People in my neighborhood already trust me and know me as a responsible dog owner.

4. Write a mission statement for your business in less than three sentences that clearly states your competitive advantage, strategy, and tactics.

   Happy Paws: We Keep Tails Waggin'!

   Our mission is to offer a quality and affordable dog walking service to busy professionals and elderly dog owners in the Victoria Park section of Detroit. Happy Paws is knowledgeable about dog training and handling. We will treat your dog with kindness, love, and respect.

Your Marketing Mix (Chapter 18)

Step One: Consumer Analysis

Describe your target consumer.

Market Segment One: Busy Professionals
Age: 30-50
Gender: Both
Income: $50,000 and up

INTERMEDIATE SAMPLE STUDENT BUSINESS PLAN: HAPPY PAWS DOG WALKING SERVICE

Market Segment Two: Homebound Elderly
Age: 70-90
Gender: Both
Income: Fixed income of $35,000 - $50,000

Step Two: Market Analysis

1. How will you look at location, population, personality, and behavior when you analyze your market segment?

   My business will service customers who live in the Victoria Park area of Detroit, Michigan. This area is approximately 7 square miles.

   My customers care deeply about their pets but they cannot walk their dogs as often as they would like due to time and physical constraints.

2. Use your market analysis method to describe your market segment. Roughly how many consumers are in this segment?

   Through the 2000 U.S. Census (online), I learned that the city of Detroit has close to one million people and 337,000 households. I am figuring that my market segment represents 1% of this total, or 3,370 households.

3. Explain how your marketing plan targets your market segment.

   I will post flyers in the establishments that people in my neighborhood use — such as the local supermarket and pet store. I plan to take my customers' dogs to the neighborhood park where other dog owners will see my business in action! I can pass out business cards to people who encounter me walking dogs on the street.

4. What percentage of your market do you feel you need to capture for your business to be profitable?

   I am estimating that 15% of the households in my neighborhood own at least one dog. That is, there are 252 dog-owning households. I would like to capture 10% of this market, which would be 25 dogs.

   However, I do not need to achieve this goal for my business to be profitable. For example, if I had a roster of 20 dogs that I walked an average of three days per week for 22 weeks per year, sales would be close to $20,000!

5. Who are the potential customers you plan to approach in the first two months of business?

   My first step in marketing will be to go to the park on the weekends and pass out business cards while I walk my own dogs. I expect to find the "busy professionals" in the park on the weekends. Targeting the seniors will be more difficult. I plan to call my local senior center to see if they can help me to get the word out about Happy Paws.

Advertising and Publicity (Chapter 19)

1. What is your business slogan?

   Happy Paws Dog Walking Service: We Keep Tails Waggin'!

2. Where do you intend to advertise?

   I will advertise once a month in my local newspaper. The ad will feature my business card and cost $30 per month.

3. Are you planning to use cause-related marketing?

   Yes. I plan to participate in the ASPCA's annual holiday fundraiser. I will use this event as an opportunity to spread the word about Happy Paws.

4. Write a sample press release for your business.

FOR IMMEDIATE RELEASE, DETROIT, MICHIGAN, AUGUST 1, 2006:

DETROIT TEEN LAUNCHES NEW DOG-WALKING BUSINESS

Today, Darius Jones, a seventeen-year-old student at Regis High School, announced the opening of his business: Happy Paws Dog Walking Service. Happy Paws' slogan is: *"We keep tails waggin'"* — and this is exactly what Jones intends to do.

Jones, who owns three dogs, a cat, and a turtle, is excited to be offering a convenient dog-walking service to busy professionals and homebound elderly customers in his Victoria Park neighborhood. According to Jones, "There are many families who don't have the time to walk their dogs. People are working later and later and the last thing they want to do is go outside in the cold after a long day at the office. My older customers have the time, but it is difficult for them to go outside, especially during our long winters. Happy Paws will help these dog owners by providing a reliable and affordable service."

This is Jones's first business venture. He is an honors student and plans to attend veterinary school after graduation. His long-term goal is to open his own veterinary clinic.

Jones plans to donate 5% of his net earnings to the local ASPCA. He will also be volunteering his time one day per month at Detroit's Mighty Mutts animal shelter. Happy Paws will operate six days per week: Mondays – Fridays from 3:30 – 6:30 PM and on Saturdays from 12 – 5 PM. Interested parties can contact Jones at (313) 555-9193 for more information about Happy Paws.

Break-Even Analysis (Chapter 20)

Perform a break-even analysis of your business.

Gross Profit per Unit = $4.00

Monthly Fixed Costs = $180.00

Monthly Break-Even Units = $180 ÷ $4 = 45

Selling (Chapter 21)

1. Describe the features and benefits of the product (or service) your business will focus on selling.

    Features: Home pickup and drop off, my extensive knowledge of dog breeds and training. I will provide snacks and toys.

    Benefits: Convenience and affordability

2. Choose three ways you will sell your product or service. Explain why you think these methods will work.

    Door-to-door sales calls: I will target households that own dogs.

    Letters of reference from my customers: I will include customer testimonials in my marketing materials. This will establish my credibility with potential customers.

    On-the-street prospects: I plan to distribute business cards and flyers to dog owners on the street.

3. Write a sales pitch for your product (or service).

    Happy Paws is a new dog walking service for dog owners in Victoria Park. I know that many of our neighbors are unable to walk their dogs as regularly as they'd like. Happy Paws can take your dog for a walk when you're tied up at the office or when it's too cold for you to go outside. My prices are affordable and, as you know, I love all dogs big and small!

4. Describe three customers you intend to pitch.

    Bill and Susan Carroll: This couple lives across the street from me. They have two small children and both work full time. They recently adopted a golden retriever puppy.

    Mrs. Earl: Mrs. Earl is my next-door neighbor. She is in her eighties and has a poodle named Delilah.

    Dan Ingersoll: Dan is single and in his early thirties. He works as a computer programmer and puts in many late hours at the office. He has two dogs — a boxer and a cocker spaniel.

Customer Service (Chapter 22)

Create a customer database for your business. Include name, e-mail, phone, fax, address, last contact, and/or last purchase. What five questions will you ask every customer?

Name:	Bill Carroll
E-mail	Bcarroll@igc.net
Phone	313-555-9943
Fax	None
Address	505 Victoria Park Drive West
Last Contact	September 1, 2005
Last Purchase	September 1, 2005

Name:	Mrs. Earl
E-mail	No e-mail
Phone	313-555-8534
Fax	None
Address	506 Victoria Park Drive West
Last Contact	September 1, 2005
Last Purchase	September 1, 2005

Name:	Dan Ingersoll
E-mail	Dan@programmingworld.com
Phone	313-555-4455
Fax	313-555-1390
Address	203 Sampson Avenue #4
Last Contact	August 15, 2005
Last Purchase	August 15, 2005

Five questions for every customer:

- Does your dog have any injuries or special needs?
- How does your dog behave around other dogs?
- Can your dog run off-leash?
- How does your dog behave around people, particularly small children?
- How can I contact you in the event of an emergency?

Business Communication (Chapter 24)

1. Which of these business communication tools will you use?

Phone:	✓
Voice mail:	✓
Fax:	

INTERMEDIATE SAMPLE STUDENT BUSINESS PLAN: HAPPY PAWS DOG WALKING SERVICE

    E-mail: ✓

    Text messaging: _____

    Other (describe): _____

2. Have you designed a letterhead for your business?

   Not yet. My invoices and marketing materials will feature my logo but I don't expect to be writing my customers letters, at least in the beginning.

Legal Structure (Chapter 25)

1. What is the legal structure of your business?

   Sole Proprietorship: ✓

   Partnership: _____

   Limited Partnership: _____

   C Corporation: _____

   Subchapter-S: _____

   Limited Liability Company: _____

   Nonprofit Corporation: _____

2. Why did you choose this structure?

   Happy Paws will be a sole proprietorship. At this time, my business is just beginning and I am the only employee. As my business grows, I would like to incorporate so that I can protect my personal assets and savings. In the short term I plan to get a good insurance policy and have each of my customers sign a waiver.

3. Who will be the partners or stockholders for your company?

   My brother Charles has a 25% equity stake in Happy Paws.

4. Have you registered your business?

   I plan to fill out my "Doing Business As" (DBA) form next week and register Happy Paws at the local courthouse.

5. Have you applied for a sales-tax identification number?

   I will file for my sales-tax ID number at the same time that I submit my "Doing Business As" form.

INTERMEDIATE SAMPLE STUDENT BUSINESS PLAN: HAPPY PAWS DOG WALKING SERVICE

Manufacturing (Chapter 26)

1. What are the zoning laws in your area? Does your business comply?

   This is not relevant to my business.

2. Do you intend to manufacture your product? If so, describe the manufacturing process you will use. If not, describe how your product is manufactured.

   This is not relevant to my business.

Production/Distribution Chain (Chapter 27)

1. How do you plan to distribute your product to your target market?

   I am not selling a concrete product. Happy Paws is a service business. I will personally deliver the service directly to customers.

2. Use this chart to show the production/distribution channel for your own business, and the markups at each point in the chain.

   This is not relevant to my business since I'm neither a manufacturer nor a wholesaler.

3. What is the estimated time between your placing an order with your supplier and the product's availability to your customers?

   As soon as customers sign up with Happy Paws, I will begin walking their dogs. With each customer, I will work out a scheduling plan. It is my priority to respond to customers quickly!

Quality (Chapter 28)

1. How will you deliver a high-quality product (service) to your customers? Describe your quality control procedure.

   Quality will be delivered when I provide customers with a reliable and affordable service. I will be on time for my customers. I will be neat and considerate when I enter people's homes to collect their dogs. I also plan to stay current on the latest dog care techniques. It is my hobby to read about different breeds so I will continue to gather as much information as I can about the types of dogs I am walking.

2. Write a motto for your business that will remind you to stay focused on quality.

   "Quality Care Always!"

Human Resources (Chapter 29)

1. Fill out a PERT Chart for your business.

HAPPY PAWS: PERT CHART (time frame in weeks)				
Task	1	2	3	4
Make flyers and business cards	✓			
Purchase classified ad			✓	
Make five door-to-door sales calls	✓	✓	✓	✓

2. Will you be hiring employees? If so, describe what their qualifications should be, what you intend to pay them, and how they will help your business.

   I do not plan to hire any employees for my first year of operations. If I find that I have more demand than I can satisfy with my own labor, then I will hire subcontractors at a rate of $10 per dog walk.

3. Provide contact information for your accountant, attorney, banker, and insurance agent.

   I don't have an accountant or an attorney. My banker is Mrs. Leila Sims at the local credit union. My insurance agent is Mr. John Davis. He is a family friend. My mother will help me with my bookkeeping.

4. What are your policies toward employees? How do you plan to make your business a positive and rewarding place to work?

   When I do hire employees, I will incentivize them by offering them commissions for signing up new customers.

5. Create an organizational chart for your business.

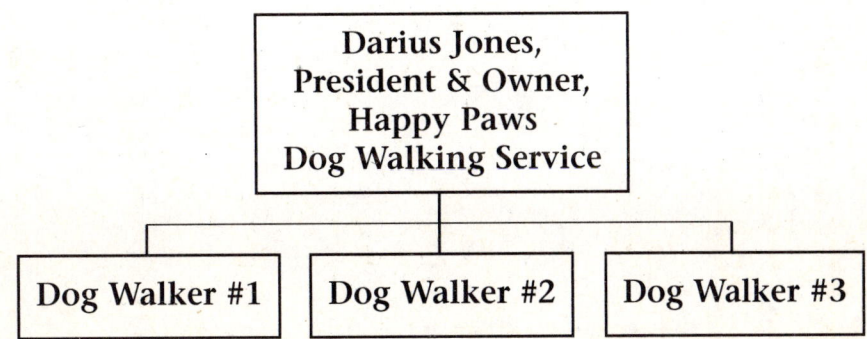

INTERMEDIATE SAMPLE STUDENT BUSINESS PLAN: HAPPY PAWS DOG WALKING SERVICE

Technology (Chapter 30)

1. Which technology tools will you use for your business, and why?

Technology Tool	Function
Cell Phone	Sales calls
	Customer care and communciation
Computer	Create flyers and business cards
	Billing and record keeping
E-mail and Internet	Customer care and communication
	Research dog care techniques and dog breed information

2. Explain how you will access this technology.

I plan to upgrade my cell phone plan by negotiating with my service provider for a better deal. My cell phone will serve as an important technology tool since it will provide an efficient way for me to communicate with my customers. I already own a computer but I plan to purchase a new printer at a local store.

Your Business Plan
Basic Module Business Plan Template

A business plan is the road map that gives a business direction.
— Joseph Mancuso, *author of* How to Write a Winning Business Plan

Now you are ready to write your final business plan by combining the ideas from the Basic, Intermediate, and Advanced Business Plan Reviews that you completed previously in this workbook. This final plan will allow you to make changes and improvements to your earlier plans.

Note to the teacher: *The CD-ROM included with your Teacher's Edition contains Microsoft® Word templates for this Q&A-format business plan and an outline-only format business plan. Students can use either template to input their business plans.*

The CD also contains a PowerPoint® presentation-format template that can be used in competitions or oral plan presentations.

BASIC MODULE: BUSINESS PLAN TEMPLATE

Your Business Idea (Chapter 1)

1. Describe your business idea.

   _____
   _____
   _____
   _____
   _____
   _____
   _____
   _____
   _____
   _____
   _____
   _____

2. What is the name of your business?

   _____
   _____

3. Explain how your idea will satisfy a consumer need.

   _____
   _____
   _____
   _____
   _____

4. Provide contact information for each owner.

   _____
   _____
   _____
   _____
   _____

BASIC MODULE: BUSINESS PLAN TEMPLATE

5. If there is more than one owner, describe how the business ownership will be shared.

Economics of One Unit (Chapter 2)

1. Do you intend to pay yourself a salary, wage, dividend, or commission? Explain.

2. What type of business are you starting?

3. Calculate the Economics of One Unit for your business.

ECONOMICS OF ONE UNIT (EOU)
Manufacturing Business: unit = _____
Selling Price per Unit: $ _____
Labor Cost per Hour: $ _____
No. of Hours per Unit: _____ $ _____
Materials per Unit: _____
Cost of Goods Sold per Unit: $ _____
Gross Profit per Unit: $ _____

BASIC MODULE: BUSINESS PLAN TEMPLATE

ECONOMICS OF ONE UNIT (EOU)

Wholesale Business: unit = _____

Selling Price per Unit:	$ _____
Cost of Goods Sold per Unit:	_____
Gross Profit per Unit:	$ _____

Retail Business: unit = _____

Selling Price per Unit:	$ _____
Cost of Goods Sold per Unit:	_____
Gross Profit per Unit:	$ _____

Service Business: unit = _____

Selling Price per Unit:	$ _____
Supplies per Unit: $ _____	
Labor Costs per Hour: _____	
Cost of Goods Sold per Unit:	$ _____
Gross Profit per Unit:	$ _____

Return on Investment (Chapter 3)

Business Goals:

1. What is your short-term business goal (less than one year)? What do you plan to invest to achieve this goal? What is your expected ROI?

_____
_____
_____
_____

2. What is your long-term business goal (from one to five years)? What do you plan to invest to achieve this goal? What is your expected ROI?

   _____
   _____
   _____
   _____

Personal Goals:

1. What is your career goal? What do you plan to invest to achieve this goal? What is your expected ROI?

   _____
   _____
   _____
   _____

2. How much education will you need for your career?

   _____
   _____
   _____
   _____

3. Have you tried to get a part-time job related to your chosen career?

   _____
   _____
   _____
   _____

Opportunity Recognition (Chapter 4)

1. What resources and skills do you (and the other owners of your business) have that will help make your business successful?

   _____
   _____

BASIC MODULE: BUSINESS PLAN TEMPLATE

2. Perform a SWOT analysis of your business.

   Type of Business: _____

   Strengths (Entrepreneur's abilities and contacts)

   _____
   _____
   _____
   _____

   Weaknesses (The problems the entrepreneur faces, from lack of money or training to lack of time or experience.)

   _____
   _____
   _____
   _____

   Opportunities (Lucky breaks or creative advantages the entrepreneur can use to get ahead of the competition.)

   _____
   _____
   _____
   _____

   Threats (Anything that might be bad for the business, from competitors to legal problems.)

   _____
   _____
   _____
   _____

Core Beliefs (Chapter 5)

1. Describe three core beliefs you will use in running your company.

   _____
   _____
   _____
   _____
   _____

2. Choose a motto for your company. (You can select or adapt from the 50 positive quotes in Chapter 5, find one elsewhere, or make up your own.)

   _____
   _____
   _____
   _____

Supply and Demand (Chapter 6)

1. What factors will influence the demand for your product or service?

   _____
   _____
   _____
   _____

2. What factors will influence the supply for your product or service?

   _____
   _____
   _____
   _____

Product Development (Chapter 7)

How do you plan to protect your product/trademark/logo? (Check one, and explain.)

_____ patent

_____ copyright

_____ trademark

Explain: _____

Competitive Advantage (Chapter 8)

1. What is your competitive advantage?

2. How will your business help others? List all organizations to which you plan to contribute. (Your contribution may be time, money, your product, or something else.)

Operating Costs (Chapter 9)

1. List and describe your monthly fixed costs.

2. List and describe your monthly variable costs.

3. Re-calculate your economics of one unit, allocating as many variable costs as possible.

ECONOMICS OF ONE UNIT (EOU)

_____ **Business:** unit = _____

Selling Price per Unit: $ _____

    Supplies/Materials: $ _____

    Labor: _____

    Cost of Goods Sold per Unit: $ _____ $ _____

    Commission: $ _____

    Packaging: _____

    Total Other Variable Costs per Unit: $ _____   _____

Total Variable Costs per Unit: $ _____   _____

Gross Profit per Unit: $ _____

4. Add a cash reserve that covers three months of fixed costs.

_____
_____
_____
_____

Marketing (Chapter 10)

1. Describe the Four P's for your business.

    Product — Why will your product meet a consumer need?

    Place — Where do you intend to sell your product?

    Price — What price do you plan to sell your product for, and why?

    Promotion — How do you plan to advertise and promote your product?

_____
_____
_____
_____

BASIC MODULE: BUSINESS PLAN TEMPLATE

2. Fill out a marketing plan for your business.

	Street Vending	Your Own Home	Door to Door	Flea Markets	School/ Community	Through local stores	Youth Clubs	Internet	Other
Business Cards									
Posters									
Flyers									
Phone Sales									
Sales Calls									
Brochures									
Mailings									
Newspaper/ Radio/TV									
Web site									
Other									

BASIC MODULE: BUSINESS PLAN TEMPLATE

3. Do you intend to publicize your philanthropy? Why or why not? If you do, explain how you will work your philanthropy into your marketing.

___
___
___
___

Market Research (Chapter 11)

1. Research your industry and display the results in a one-page report that includes pie charts and bar or line graphs. Describe your target market within the industry. Use separate paper for this exercise.

2. Describe your market segment and the results of your research on this market segment.

___
___
___
___
___
___
___

Record Keeping (Chapter 12)

1. Describe your record-keeping system.

___
___
___
___
___

2. List all bank accounts you will open for your business.

___
___
___

BASIC MODULE: BUSINESS PLAN TEMPLATE

Projected Income Statement (Chapter 13)

1. Complete a monthly projected budget and one-year income statement for your business.

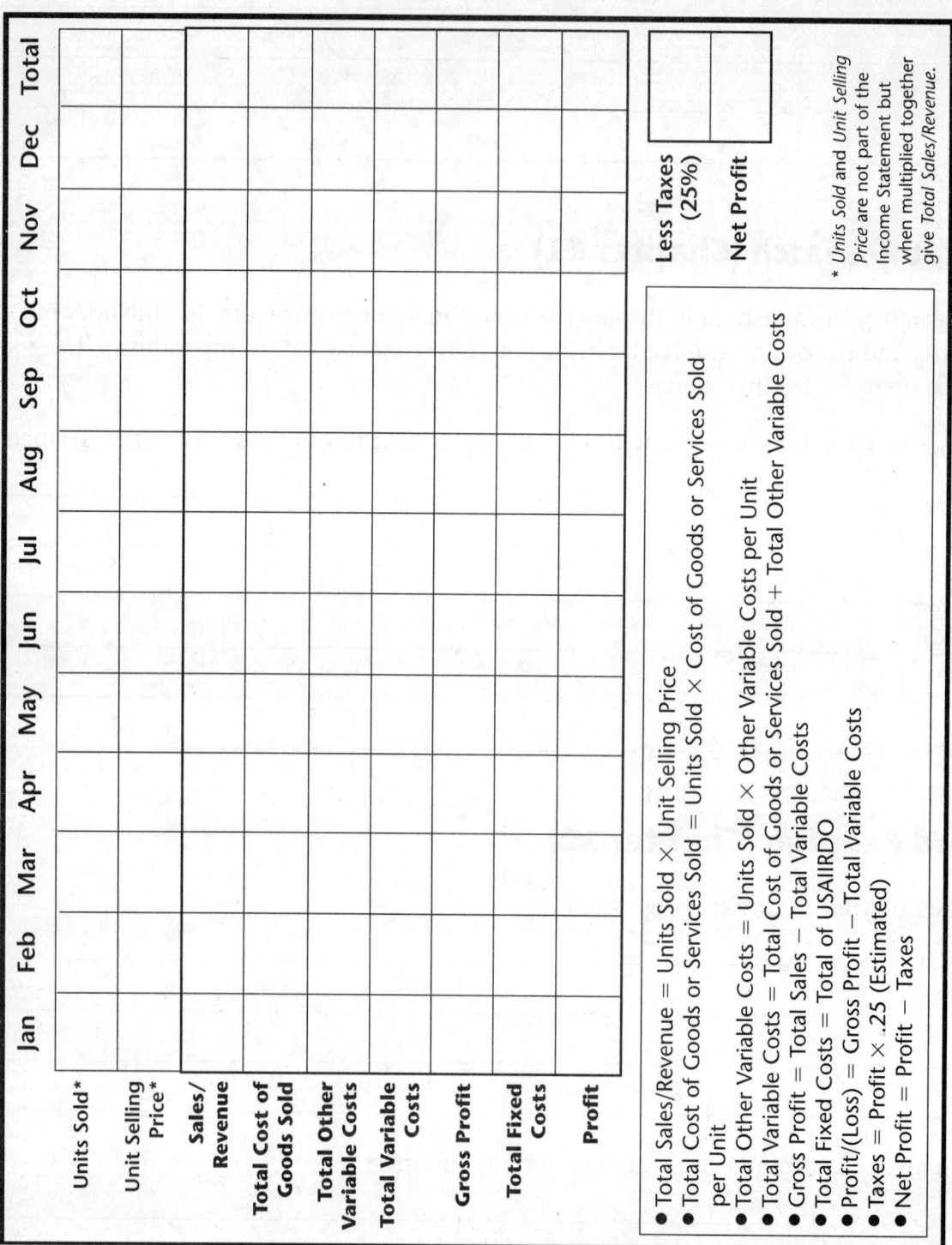

2. Use your projected one-year income statement to calculate:

   Projected ROI for one year: _____ %; Projected ROS for one year: _____ %

410

Financing Strategy (Chapter 14)

1. What legal structure have you chosen for your business? Why?
   _____
   _____
   _____
   _____

2. List the cost of the items you will need to buy to start your business.
   _____
   _____
   _____
   _____

3. Add up the items to get your total start-up capital.

Item	Where will you buy this?	Cost

   Estimated Total Start-Up Costs: $ _____

4. Add a cash reserve of three months' fixed costs.
   _____
   _____
   _____

BASIC MODULE: BUSINESS PLAN TEMPLATE

5. List the sources of financing for your start-up capital. Identify whether each source is equity, debt, or a gift. Indicate the amount and type for each source.

Source	Equity	Debt	Gift
Personal savings:	_____	_____	_____
Relatives:	_____	_____	_____
Friends:	_____	_____	_____
Investors:	_____	_____	_____
Grants:	_____	_____	_____
Other:	_____	_____	_____
Subtotal:	_____	_____	_____

    Total Equity + Total Debt + Total Gift = Total Financing : _____

    If you use equity financing, what percentage of ownership will you give up?
    _____
    _____
    _____
    _____

    If you use debt financing, what is the maximum interest rate you will pay?
    _____
    _____
    _____
    _____

6. What is your debt ratio? What is your debt-to-equity ratio?
    _____
    _____
    _____
    _____
    _____

BASIC MODULE: BUSINESS PLAN TEMPLATE

7. What is your payback period? In other words, how long will it take you to earn enough profit to cover start-up capital?
_____
_____

Negotiation (Chapter 15)

Describe any suppliers with whom you will have to negotiate.
_____
_____
_____
_____
_____

Buying Wholesale (Chapter 16)

1. Where will you purchase the products you plan to sell, or the products you plan to use to manufacture the products you will be selling?

Name of Supplier/Item	Price
_____	$ _____
_____	$ _____
_____	$ _____
_____	$ _____
_____	$ _____
_____	$ _____

2. Have you applied for a sales-tax ID number?
_____
_____

BASIC MODULE: BUSINESS PLAN TEMPLATE

Business Plan Notes

Your Business Plan
Intermediate Module Business Plan Template

INTERMEDIATE MODULE: BUSINESS PLAN TEMPLATE

Your Competitive Strategy (Chapter 17)

1. Use the following charts to define your business, analyze your competitive advantage, and determine your tactics.

Business Definition Question	Response
1. *The Offer:* What products and services will be sold by the business?	1.
2. *Target Market:* Which consumer segment will the business focus on?	2.
3. *Production Capability:* How will that offer be produced and delivered to those customers?	3.

Competitive Advantage Question	Competitive Difference (USP)
1. *The Offer:* What will be better or different about the products and services that will be sold by the business?	1.
2. *Target Market:* What customers should be the focus of the business, to make it as successful as possible?	2.
3. *Production and Delivery Capability:* What will be better or different about the way that offer is produced and delivered to those customers?	3.

INTERMEDIATE MODULE: BUSINESS PLAN TEMPLATE

Tactical Question	Issues	Solutions
1. *Sales Plan:* Where and how will you sell to your customers?	How to identify prospects and convert them to sales.	
2. *Market Communications:* How will you communicate with your customers and make them aware of your business offer?	How to make customers aware of your offer; how to attract them to the business.	
3. *Operating Plan:* How will you manage your internal operations?	How to make the business go, and determine who will perform the tasks.	
4. *Budget:* How do you plan to manage your revenues and expenses?	What are the sources of revenue? What are the items that have to be purchased?	

INTERMEDIATE MODULE: BUSINESS PLAN TEMPLATE

2. Describe your strategy for outperforming the competition.
   _____
   _____
   _____
   _____

3. What tactics will you use to carry out this strategy?
   _____
   _____
   _____
   _____

4. Write a mission statement for your business in less than three sentences that clearly states your competitive advantage, strategy, and tactics.
   _____
   _____
   _____
   _____
   _____

Your Marketing Mix (Chapter 18)

Step One: Consumer Analysis

1. Describe your market segment.
   _____
   _____
   _____
   _____

2. Describe your target consumer: age: _____

   gender: _____

   income: _____

Step Two: Market Analysis

1. How will you look at location, population, personality, and behavior when you analyze your market segment?

   _____
   _____
   _____
   _____

2. Use your market analysis method to describe your market segment. Roughly how many consumers are in this segment?

   _____
   _____
   _____
   _____

3. Explain how your marketing plan targets your market segment.

   _____
   _____
   _____
   _____

4. What percentage of your market do you feel you need to capture for your business to be profitable?

   _____
   _____
   _____
   _____

5. Who are the potential customers you plan to approach in the first two months of business?

   _____
   _____
   _____
   _____

INTERMEDIATE MODULE: BUSINESS PLAN TEMPLATE

Step Three: The Marketing Mix

1. Describe The Four P's for your business.

    Product — How will your product meet a consumer need?
    _____
    _____
    _____
    _____

    Price — Are your prices competitive? Do a comparison. What price do you plan to sell your product for, and why? What is your pricing strategy?
    _____
    _____
    _____
    _____

    Place — Describe your business location and its competitive advantages.
    _____
    _____
    _____
    _____

    Promotion — How do you plan to advertise and promote your product?
    _____
    _____
    _____
    _____

2. Fill out the following marketing plan for your business.

INTERMEDIATE MODULE: BUSINESS PLAN TEMPLATE

	Street Vending	Your Own Home	Door to Door	Flea Markets	School/ Community	Through local stores	Youth Clubs	Internet	Other
Business Cards									
Posters									
Flyers									
Phone Sales									
Sales Calls									
Brochures									
Mailings									
Newspaper/ Radio/TV									
Web site									
Other									

INTERMEDIATE MODULE: BUSINESS PLAN TEMPLATE

Advertising and Publicity (Chapter 19)

1. What is your business slogan?

2. Where do you intend to advertise?

3. How do you plan to get publicity for your business?

4. Are you planning to use cause-related marketing?

5. Write a sample press release for your business. Use separate paper for this exercise.

Break-Even Analysis (Chapter 20)

Perform a break-even analysis of your business.

INTERMEDIATE MODULE: BUSINESS PLAN TEMPLATE

Break-Even Units per Month for your business = _____

Selling (Chapter 21)

1. Describe the features and benefits of the product (or service) your business will focus on selling.

Features	Benefits

2. Choose three ways you will sell your product or service. Explain why you think these methods will work.

3. Write a sales pitch for your product (or service).

> **INTERMEDIATE MODULE: BUSINESS PLAN TEMPLATE**

4. Describe three customers you intend to pitch.

   _____
   _____
   _____
   _____

Customer Service (Chapter 22)

Create a customer database for your business. Include name, e-mail, phone, fax, address, last contact, and/or last purchase. What five questions will you ask every customer?

a. _____

b. _____

c. _____

d. _____

e. _____

Name	E-mail	Phone	Fax	Address	Last contact	Last purchase

Business Math (Chapter 23)

Double-check all of the math and financial information in your business plan to be sure it is accurate.

INTERMEDIATE MODULE: BUSINESS PLAN TEMPLATE

Business Communication (Chapter 24)

1. Which of these business communication tools will you use?

   Phone: _____

   Voice mail: _____

   Fax: _____

   E-mail: _____

   Text messaging: _____

   Other (describe): _____

2. Have you designed a letterhead for your business?
   _____

Legal Structure (Chapter 25)

1. What is the legal structure of your business?

   Sole Proprietorship: _____

   Partnership: _____

   Limited Partnership: _____

   C Corporation: _____

   Subchapter-S: _____

   Limited Liability Company: _____

   Nonprofit Corporation: _____

2. Why did you choose this structure?
   _____
   _____
   _____
   _____

INTERMEDIATE MODULE: BUSINESS PLAN TEMPLATE

3. Who will be the partners or stockholders for your company?

   _____
   _____
   _____
   _____

4. Have you registered your business?

   _____
   _____

5. Have you applied for a sales-tax identification number?

   _____
   _____

Manufacturing (Chapter 26)

1. What are the zoning laws in your area? Does your business comply?

   _____
   _____
   _____
   _____

2. Do you intend to manufacture your product? If so, describe the manufacturing process you will use. If not, describe how your product is manufactured.

   _____
   _____
   _____
   _____
   _____
   _____

INTERMEDIATE MODULE: BUSINESS PLAN TEMPLATE

Production/Distribution Chain (Chapter 27)

1. How do you plan to distribute your product to your target market?

   _____
   _____
   _____
   _____

2. Use this chart to show the production/distribution channel for your own business, and the markups at each point in the chain.

   Manufacturer: Name: _____
   Contact information: _____
   _____

   Markup: $ _____ Markup: % _____

   Wholesaler: Name: _____
   Contact information: _____
   _____

   Markup: $ _____ Markup: % _____

   Retailer (You): Name: _____
   Name: _____
   Contact information: _____
   _____

   Markup: $ _____ Markup: % _____

3. What is the estimated time between your placing an order with your supplier and the product's availability to your customers?

   _____
   _____
   _____
   _____

INTERMEDIATE MODULE: BUSINESS PLAN TEMPLATE

Quality (Chapter 28)

1. How will you deliver a high-quality product (service) to your customers? Describe your quality control procedure.

   _____
   _____
   _____
   _____

2. Write a motto for your business that will remind you to stay focused on quality.

   _____
   _____
   _____
   _____

Human Resources (Chapter 29)

1. Fill out the PERT Chart on the following page for your business.

2. Will you be hiring employees? If so, describe what their qualifications should be, what you intend to pay them, and how they will help your business.

   _____
   _____
   _____
   _____
   _____
   _____
   _____
   _____
   _____
   _____

INTERMEDIATE MODULE: BUSINESS PLAN TEMPLATE

SAMPLE PERT CHART (TIME FRAME IN WEEKS)						
Task	1	2	3	4	5	6
Writing Business Plan						
Financing						
Developing Product						
Finding Location						
Hiring Workers						
Setting Up Office						
Other						

3. Provide contact information for your accountant, attorney, banker, and insurance agent.

Accountant: _____

_____

_____

Attorney: _____

_____

_____

Banker: _____

_____

_____

INTERMEDIATE MODULE: BUSINESS PLAN TEMPLATE

Insurance Agent: _____
_____
_____

4. What are your policies toward employees? How do you plan to make your business a positive and rewarding place to work?

   _____
   _____
   _____
   _____
   _____
   _____
   _____
   _____
   _____
   _____

5. Create an organizational chart for your business. Use separate paper if you need additional space.

INTERMEDIATE MODULE: BUSINESS PLAN TEMPLATE

Technology (Chapter 30)

1. Which technology tools will you use for your business, and why?

	Yes	No	Why?/Why not?
Computer	___	___	_____
Home Page (Web site)	___	___	_____
Calculator	___	___	_____
Electronic Organizer	___	___	_____
Accounting Software	___	___	_____
Mail-Order Software	___	___	_____
Online Service	___	___	_____
Instant Investment News	___	___	_____
E-mail and Newsgroups	___	___	_____
Print, Audio, and Video Brochures	___	___	_____
Mailing Lists	___	___	_____
Electronic Storefront	___	___	_____
Business Plan Software	___	___	_____
Computerized Visuals	___	___	_____
24-Hour Banking	___	___	_____
Tax-Preparation Software	___	___	_____
Other _____	___	___	_____
Other _____	___	___	_____
Other _____	___	___	_____
Other _____	___	___	_____
Other _____	___	___	_____
Other _____	___	___	_____

INTERMEDIATE MODULE: BUSINESS PLAN TEMPLATE

2. Write a memo explaining how you will access this technology.

Your Business Plan
Advanced Module Business Plan Template

ADVANCED MODULE: BUSINESS PLAN TEMPLATE

Raising Capital (Chapter 31)

1. Describe financing sources that might be willing to invest in your business in exchange for equity.

    Friends and family: _____

    "Angels": _____

    MESBICs: _____

2. What other financing sources would be willing to invest in your business in exchange for equity?

    _____
    _____
    _____

Corporations (Chapter 32)

1. Is your business a: C Corporation _____

    Subchapter-S _____

    Limited Liability Company (LLC) _____

    Nonprofit Corporation _____

2. Why did you choose this corporate structure?

    _____
    _____
    _____
    _____

3. Who are the stockholders of your corporation?

    _____
    _____
    _____
    _____

4. Who is on your board of directors?

Stocks (Chapter 33)

1. If your business is incorporated, describe what percentage of your company is represented by one share of stock.

2. Is your corporation's stock publicly or privately held?

Bonds (Chapter 34)

1. Do you intend to use debt to finance your business? Explain.

> **ADVANCED MODULE: BUSINESS PLAN TEMPLATE**

2. Would you ever issue bonds to finance your business?

   _____
   _____
   _____
   _____

Your Balance Sheet (Chapter 35)

1. Create a Projected Balance Sheet for your business for one year.

BALANCE SHEET			
Assets		**Liabilities**	
Cash:	$ _____	Short-Term Liabilities:	$ _____
Inventory:	_____	Long-Term Liabilities:	_____
Capital Equipment:	_____		
Other Assets:	_____	Owner's Equity:	$ _____
Total Assets:	$ _____	**Total Liabilities + OE:**	$ _____

2. Create a pie chart showing your assets, short-term liabilities, long-term liabilities, and owner's equity.

3. What is your debt ratio?

   _____
   _____
   _____

4. What is your debt-to-equity ratio?

Venture Capital (Chapter 36)

Have you found any sources of venture capital that you intend to contact? Describe.

Contracts (Chapter 37)

1. What is the most important contract you will need to run your business?

2. Describe any additional contracts you have, or plan to secure.

3. Who is your attorney?

ADVANCED MODULE: BUSINESS PLAN TEMPLATE

Socially Responsible Business (Chapter 38)

1. Choose three of the ways below you would use to run a socially responsible business.

    Recycling paper, glass, and plastic. _____

    Donating a portion of profits to a nonprofit. _____

    Not using animals to test products. _____

    Offering employees incentives to volunteer in the community. _____

    Establishing a safe and healthy workplace. _____

    Other. _____
    _____
    _____

2. What cause-related marketing do you intend to use? How will this support and reinforce your competitive advantage?

    _____
    _____
    _____
    _____
    _____

Small Business and Government (Chapter 39)

What laws — such as minimum wage and age requirements, health and safety regulations, or anti-discrimination laws — will affect your business?

_____
_____
_____
_____
_____

ADVANCED MODULE: BUSINESS PLAN TEMPLATE

Building Good Personal and Business Credit (Chapter 40)

1. My *personal* credit history is:

    Bad _____

    Good _____

    Not yet established _____

    Describe how you plan to establish good personal credit.

    _____

    _____

    _____

2. My *business* credit history is:

    Bad _____

    Good _____

    Not yet established _____

    Describe how you plan to establish good business credit.

    _____

    _____

    _____

Cash Flow (Chapter 41)

1. Use the cash flow chart on the next page to create a projected cash flow statement for your business for one year.

2. Calculate the "burn rate" for your business.

    _____

    _____

    _____

ADVANCED MODULE: BUSINESS PLAN TEMPLATE

NFTE CASH FLOW STATEMENT

Business: _____   Date: _____

Beginning Cash Balance: $ _____

    Cash Inflow
        Investment: $ _____
        Sales: _____
    Total Cash Inflow: $ _____

    Cash Outflow
        Inventory: $ _____
        Variable Costs: _____
        Fixed Costs: _____
        Equipment: _____
        Other Outflows: _____
    Total Cash Outflow: $ _____   _____

Net Cash Flow: _____
Ending Cash Balance: $ _____

---

3. Use your projected balance sheet (Chapter 35) to calculate your working capital.

_____

_____

_____

_____

Intellectual Property (Chapter 42)

1. Describe any intellectual property you are developing for your business.

_____

_____

_____

_____

ADVANCED MODULE: BUSINESS PLAN TEMPLATE

2. How do you intend to protect your intellectual property? Explain why it qualifies for this protection.

   _____
   _____
   _____
   _____

Ethical Business Behavior (Chapter 43)

1. Describe the corporate governance plan for your business. It should include five policies (rules) that will be the backbone of your company's ethics.

   _____
   _____
   _____
   _____
   _____
   _____
   _____
   _____
   _____
   _____

2. Provide information on each of your mentors or advisors. If there will be a board of advisors, list each member and describe his or her commitment to the business.

   _____
   _____
   _____
   _____
   _____
   _____
   _____

ADVANCED MODULE: BUSINESS PLAN TEMPLATE

Taxation (Chapter 44)

Which tax forms will you have to fill out for your business? Check all that apply.

    1040 U.S. Individual Tax Return   _____

    Schedule C, Profit or Loss from Business   _____

    Schedule SE, Self-Employment Tax   _____

    Quarterly Sales and Use Tax Return   _____

Insurance (Chapter 45)

1. What types of insurance will your business need? Explain.

   _____

   _____

   _____

   _____

2. Describe the premium, deductible, and payout for each policy you plan to carry.

   _____

   _____

   _____

   _____

Franchising and Licensing (Chapter 46)

Do you plan to franchise your business, or license any of your products? Explain.

_____

_____

_____

_____

ADVANCED MODULE: BUSINESS PLAN TEMPLATE

International Opportunities (Chapter 47)

1. Are there customers for your business in other countries? How do you plan to reach them?
   _____
   _____
   _____
   _____
   _____

2. Describe any international competitors you have found who may be able to access your customers. How do you intend to compete?
   _____
   _____
   _____
   _____
   _____
   _____
   _____
   _____

Investment Goals and Risk Tolerance (Chapter 48)

1. I plan to save _____ % of my net income to achieve personal financial goals.

2. My primary financial goal is _____.

3. My investment risk tolerance is _____.

Investing for a Secure Future (Chapter 49)

1. I will invest my savings as follows:

   Current Cash Value   **Investment Mix**

   Stocks $ _____   Stocks   _____ %

   Bonds $ _____   Bonds   _____ %

   Cash $ _____   Cash   _____ %

ADVANCED MODULE: BUSINESS PLAN TEMPLATE

2. My weighted average ROI is: _____
   _____
   _____
   _____

3. Using the Rule of 72, the number of years it will take my portfolio to double is: _____ years.
   _____
   _____

Exit Strategy (Chapter 50)

1. Describe your exit strategy.
   _____
   _____
   _____
   _____
   _____
   _____
   _____
   _____
   _____

2. Why will this exit strategy be attractive to potential investors?
   _____
   _____
   _____
   _____
   _____
   _____
   _____

NFTE Record Keeping System

NFTE Journal - 10 ©

Company: _____
Student Name: _____
Class / Section: _____
Teacher: _____

Month / Year: _____

(hint: Write the month and year large so it's easy to see.)

Cash is an ASSET

Ck No.	DATE	TO / FROM	FOR - With Number Details	DEPOSIT $ IN	PAYMENT $ OUT	BALANCE FORWARD
						-
1						
2						
3						
4						
5						
6						
7						
8						
9						
10						
11						
12						
13						
14						
15						
16						
17						
18						
19						
20						
21						
22						
23						
24						
25						
26						
27						
28						
29						
30						

1- If sales tax is collected in addition to selling price, it should be included in REVENUE. Sales tax will be calculated by multiplying REVENUE times the imputed sales tax rate for your State.
2- Only income taxes (on profit) are included on this line. Other taxes are included as business expenses.
3- Taxes owed, but not yet paid should be included in the total of Short-term Liabilities. When they are paid, Short-term Liabilities should be reduced by the amount paid.
4- Cost of Goods Sold (COGS) is the same as Cost of Services Sold (COSS) for a service business. Money spent on direct labor and materials (INVENTORY) is not a "cost" until it's sold, when it becomes COGS.
5- SALES is a synonym for (means the same thing as) REVENUE.
6- The dash symbol " - " stands for " 0 " (zero) in Accounting.

NFTE

Declare COGS when Revenue is received. Use the COGS value from EOU's

Inventory is an ASSET
Capital Equipment is an ASSET

	$ IN	$ OUT	$ OUT	$ OUT	$ OUT		
INVESTMENT (equity)	REVENUE [1]	COGS [4] (COSS)	INVENTORY (purchases)	VARIABLE COSTS	FIXED COSTS	CAPITAL EQUIP'T	OTHER COSTS	EXPLANATION - Always explain OTHER COSTS entries.
1,000.00								

Note: Total each column before starting to make financial reports.

CHANGE of INVENTORY

_____ $ spent on INVENTORY
_____ minus COGS
_____ equals CHANGE of INVENTORY

Inventory is an ASSET

INCOME STATEMENT   Period: _____

REVENUE
    COGS
    Variable Costs (VC)
GROSS PROFIT
FIXED OPERATING COSTS
1.   Fixed Costs (FC)
2.   Other Costs (Except taxes on profit) [6]
    TOTAL FIXED OPERATING COSTS
    PRE-TAX PROFIT
3.   Taxes (on profit) [2] @20% (Estimated)
4.   **NET PROFIT**

STARTING BALANCE SHEET   Date: _____

5.
6. **ASSETS**
7.   Cash
8.   Inventory
9.   Capital Equipment
10.   Other Assets
11. **TOTAL ASSETS**
12. **LIABILITIES**
13.   Short-term Liabilities [3]
14.   Long-term Liabilities
15.   OWNER'S EQUITY (OE)
16. **TOTAL LIABILITIES + OE**
17. Check here ____ if ASSETS = LIABILITIES + OE

ENDING BALANCE SHEET   Date: _____

18.
19. **ASSETS**
20.   Cash
21.   Inventory
22.   Capital Equipment
23.   Other Assets
24. **TOTAL ASSETS**
25. **LIABILITIES**
26.   Short-term Liabilities [3]
27.   Long-term Liabilities
28.   OWNER'S EQUITY (OE)
29. **TOTAL LIABILITIES + OE**
30. Check here ____ if ASSETS = LIABILITIES + OE

RET. ON INVESTMENT (ROI)   Period: _____
Net Income ÷ Investment = **ROI (Month)**
Month ROI × 12 = **ROI (Annualized)**

RET. ON SALES (ROS) [5]   Period: _____
Net Income ÷ Sales = **ROS (Month)**

NFTE Journal - 10 ©

Company: _____
Student Name: _____
Class / Section: _____
Teacher: _____

Month / Year: _____

(hint: Write the month and year large so it's easy to see.)

Cash is an ASSET

Ck No.	DATE	TO / FROM	FOR - With Number Details	DEPOSIT $ IN	PAYMENT $ OUT	BALANCE FORWARD
						-
1						1
2						2
3						3
4						4
5						5
6						6
7						7
8						8
9						9
10						10
11						11
12						12
13						13
14						14
15						15
16						16
17						17
18						18
19						19
20						20
21						21
22						22
23						23
24						24
25						25
26						26
27						27
28						28
29						29
30						30

1- If sales tax is collected in addition to selling price, it should be included in REVENUE. Sales tax will be calculated by multiplying REVENUE times the imputed sales tax rate for your State.
2- Only income taxes (on profit) are included on this line. Other taxes are included as business expenses.
3- Taxes owed, but not yet paid should be included in the total of Short-term Liabilities. When they are paid, Short-term Liabilities should be reduced by the amount paid.
4- Cost of Goods Sold (COGS) is the same as Cost of Services Sold (COSS) for a service business. Money spent on direct labor and materials (INVENTORY) is not a "cost" until it's sold, when it becomes COGS.
5- SALES is a synonym for (means the same thing as) REVENUE.
6- The dash symbol " - " stands for " 0 " (zero) in Accounting.

NFTE Financial Statements Worksheet

Declare COGS when Revenue is received. Use the COGS value from EOU's

Inventory is an ASSET
Capital Equipment is an ASSET

$ IN	$ IN	$ OUT	$ OUT	$ OUT	$ OUT		
INVESTMENT (equity)	REVENUE[1]	COGS[4] (COSS)	INVENTORY (purchases)	VARIABLE COSTS	FIXED COSTS	CAPITAL EQUIP'T	OTHER COSTS	EXPLANATION - Always explain OTHER COSTS entries.
1,000.00								

CHANGE of INVENTORY
_____ $ spent on INVENTORY
minus COGS
equals CHANGE of INVENTORY

Inventory is an ASSET

INCOME STATEMENT   Period: _____

REVENUE
- COGS
- Variable Costs (VC)

GROSS PROFIT

FIXED OPERATING COSTS
1. Fixed Costs (FC)
2. Other Costs (Except taxes on profit)[6]

TOTAL FIXED OPERATING COSTS

PRE-TAX PROFIT
3. Taxes (on profit)[2] @ 20% (Estimated)

4. **NET PROFIT**

STARTING BALANCE SHEET   Date: _____

5.
ASSETS
6.
7. Cash
8. Inventory
9. Capital Equipment
10. Other Assets
11.
12. **TOTAL ASSETS**

LIABILITIES
13.
14. Short-term Liabilities[3]
15. Long-term Liabilities
16. OWNER'S EQUITY (OE)
17. **TOTAL LIABILITIES + OE**
18. Check here _____ if ASSETS = LIABILITIES + OE

ENDING BALANCE SHEET   Date: _____

ASSETS
19.
20. Cash
21. Inventory
22. Capital Equipment
23. Other Assets
24.
25. **TOTAL ASSETS**

LIABILITIES
26.
27. Short-term Liabilities[3]
28. Long-term Liabilities
29. OWNER'S EQUITY (OE)
30. **TOTAL LIABILITIES + OE**
Check here _____ if ASSETS = LIABILITIES + OE

Note: Total each column before starting to make financial reports.

RET. ON INVESTMENT (ROI)   Period: _____
Net Income ÷ Investment = ROI (Month)
Month ROI × 12 = ROI (Annualized)

RET. ON SALES (ROS)[5]   Period: _____
Net Income ÷ Sales = ROS (Month)

NFTE Journal - 10 ©

Company: _____
Student Name: _____
Class / Section: _____
Teacher: _____

Month / Year: _____

(hint: Write the month and year large so it's easy to see.)

Cash is an ASSET

Ck No.	DATE	TO / FROM	FOR - With Number Details	DEPOSIT $ IN	PAYMENT $ OUT	BALANCE FORWARD
						-
1						1
2						2
3						3
4						4
5						5
6						6
7						7
8						8
9						9
10						10
11						11
12						12
13						13
14						14
15						15
16						16
17						17
18						18
19						19
20						20
21						21
22						22
23						23
24						24
25						25
26						26
27						27
28						28
29						29
30						30

1- If sales tax is collected in addition to selling price, it should be included in REVENUE. Sales tax will be calculated by multiplying REVENUE times the imputed sales tax rate for your State.
2- Only income taxes (on profit) are included on this line. Other taxes are included as business expenses.
3- Taxes owed, but not yet paid should be included in the total of Short-term Liabilities. When they are paid, Short-term Liabilities should be reduced by the amount paid.
4- Cost of Goods Sold (COGS) is the same as Cost of Services Sold (COSS) for a service business. Money spent on direct labor and materials (INVENTORY) is not a "cost" until it's sold, when it becomes COGS.
5- SALES is a synonym for (means the same thing as) REVENUE.
6- The dash symbol " - " stands for " 0 " (zero) in Accounting.

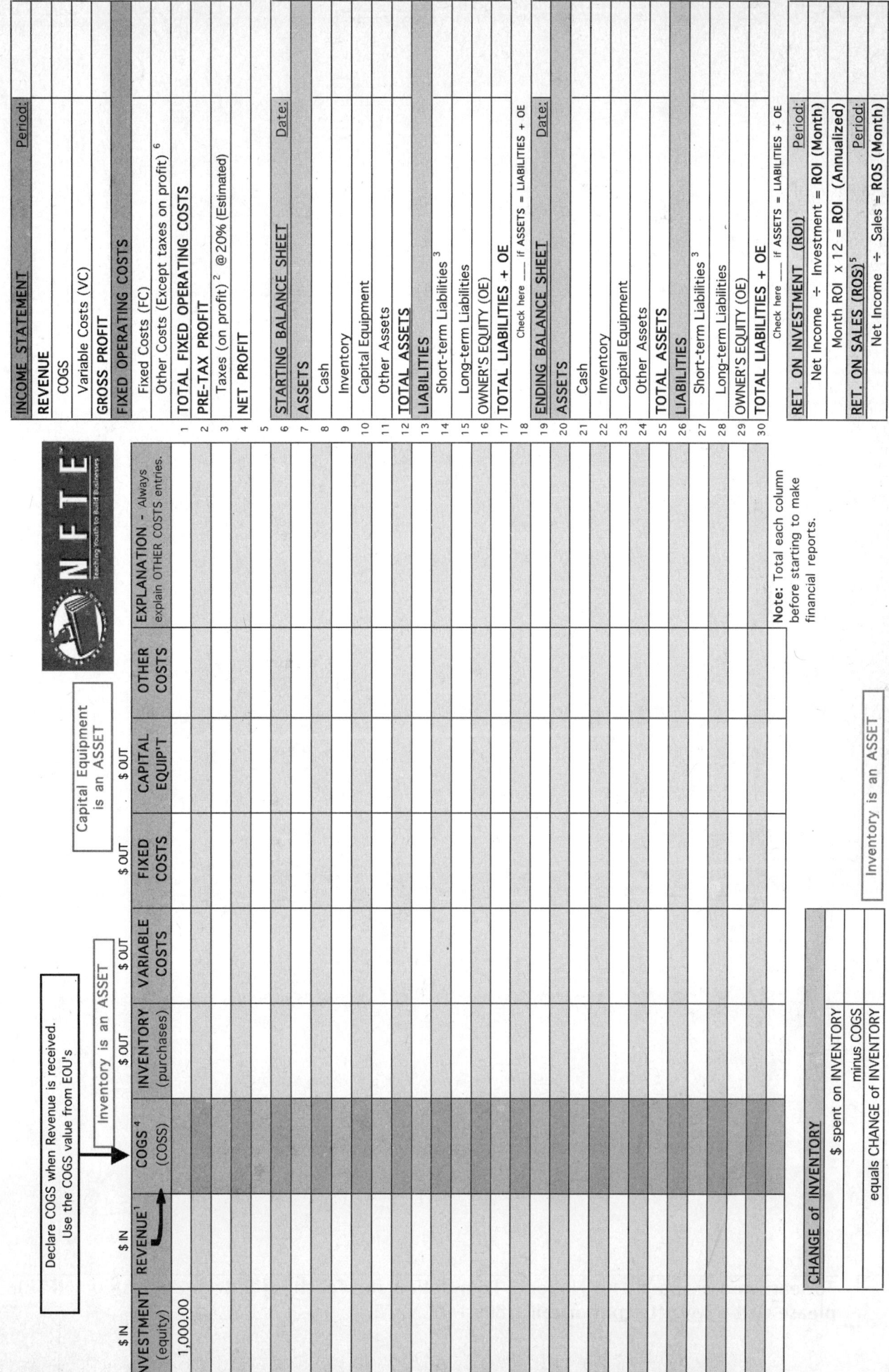

To learn more about The National Foundation for Teaching Entrepreneurship (NFTE), please visit www.nfte.com or call 1-800-FOR.NFTE.